Essays for School Students

Author
Nikita Wadi
Gayatri Chetal

V&S PUBLISHERS

Published by:

V&S PUBLISHERS

F-2/16, Ansari road, Daryaganj, New Delhi-110002
☎ 23240026, 23240027 • *Fax:* 011-23240028
Email: info@vspublishers.com • *Website:* www.vspublishers.com

Regional Office : Hyderabad

5-1-707/1, Brij Bhawan (Beside Central Bank of India Lane)
Bank Street, Koti, Hyderabad - 500 095
☎ 040-24737290
E-mail: vspublishershyd@gmail.com

Branch Office : Mumbai

Jaywant Industrial Estate, 1st Floor–108, Tardeo Road
Opposite Sobo Central Mall, Mumbai – 400 034
☎ 022-23510736
E-mail: vspublishersmum@gmail.com

BUY OUR BOOKS FROM: AMAZON FLIPKART

© **Copyright:** V&S PUBLISHERS
ISBN 978-93-579419-3-8
Edition 2020

DISCLAIMER

While every attempt has been made to provide accurate and timely information in this book, neither the author nor the publisher assumes any responsibility for errors, unintended omissions or commissions detected therein. The author and publisher make no representation or warranty with respect to the comprehensiveness or completeness of the contents provided.

All matters included have been simplified under professional guidance for general information only without any warranty for applicability on an individual. Any mention of an organization or a website in the book by way of citation or as a source of additional information doesn't imply the endorsement of the content either by the author or the publisher. It is possible that websites cited may have changed or removed between the time of editing and publishing the book.

Results from using the expert opinion in this book will be totally dependent on individual circumstances and factors beyond the control of the author and the publisher.

It makes sense to elicit advice from well informed sources before implementing the ideas given in the book. The reader assumes full responsibility for the consequences arising out from reading this book. For proper guidance, it is advisable to read the book under the watchful eyes of parents/guardian. The purchaser of this book assumes all responsibility for the use of given materials and information. The copyright of the entire content of this book rests with the author/publisher. Any infringement/ transmission of the cover design, text or illustrations, in any form, by any means, by any entity will invite legal action and be responsible for consequences thereon.

Publisher's Note

V&S Publishers is pleased to bring out the book **Essays for School Students** which enrich the knowledge of students on various burning issues at national and international level, polity and governance, Indian culture and society, science, technology and environment. The book has interesting facts on sports and games and describes about great personalities and various community helpers. It helps students know how to write letters and emails with their types and patterns with examples. This book with all genres of general awareness meets specific needs of students and aspirants of entrance exams as well. Not only does the book spreads awareness but also provides a deep insight into the facts on a topic. The book has been strategically planned in order to be user friendly. It has been designed to fulfil the quest for knowledge on different areas of study and covers up-to-date knowledge on important topics.

We hope that the book will be of immense help to the students and readers to enhance their knowledge on various topics of general knowledge. A regular revision of all the topics covered in the book is advised to refresh the level of knowledge.

We wish all students and aspirants good luck for their future endeavours.

CONTENTS

Science, Technology and Environment

Community Helpers

Visits and Journeys

Games and Sports

SECTION B : LETTERS

SECTION C : E-MAILS

SECTION – A
ESSAYS

1

GREEN REVOLUTION

Green revolution is defined as the set of technological improvements such as implementation of High Yielding Variety(HYVP) through expansion of the farming area, double-cropping, and utilisation of high yielding variety seeds for cereals, specifically for dwarf wheat and rice plants, chemical fertilizers and agro-chemicals, controlled water-supply with improved irrigation methods like drip irrigation etc. and new techniques of cultivation, including mechanization made in the agricultural sector between the 1930s and 1960s. It brought about significant improvements in the agricultural sector by increasing the production required to make India self sufficient in food grains and other crops like sugarcane, oilseeds, pulses, jute and cotton. Prior to India, the technique was adopted by various other countries like Mexico, Taiwan and Brazil but, none recorded such level of success that India did during the time.

Norman Borlaug was the name behind this revolution that outnumbered India in the food grain production. He was proudly known as the "Father of Green Revolution" and was honoured with the Noble Prize in 1960 for saving billions of people dying out of starvation and hunger.

At the time of independence, in spite of trade and other restrictions on export and import due to fear of competition from the outside world, Indian government and the Ford Foundation joined forces to import wheat from International Maize and Wheat Improvement Center (CIMMYT). Initially the state of Punjab was selected to be the first site to try the new crops production due to the availability of water sources and its success in agricultural sector in the past. As a result, the rice yields in India increased to about two tons per hectare in the 1960s; by the mid-1990s, the production rose to six tons per hectare and soon India became one of the world's most successful rice producers in the world. It became the largest exporter of food grains in the world from being an importer and presently, it is the major rice exporter, shipping approximately 4.5 million tons in 2006.

Green revolution had a widespread impact on the development of the economy. It not only sufficed self sufficiency in the country but also created plenty of job opportunities in the agricultural and industrial sector by creating dams, establishing factories, hydro-electric power stations, etc for enhancing the water supply and led to improvement in the living standards of the rural people. Indian government was able to pay back the entire loan taken from the World Bank and other affiliates, thereby improving the credit worthiness of the country outdoors.

In one of the speeches, Manmohan Singh outlined the contribution of green revolution in the growth of the nation by stating the estimated increment in the percentage of GDP due to its introduction (about 7%). It led to decrease in the poverty ratio of the country, thereby making them economically stable. Efforts are still being made to adopt improved technologies for the expansion of the agricultural sector and the relative output. The government of India also provides subsidies to the farmers on the purchase of seeds, fertilisers, pesticides and other farm equipments. Also, they are motivated to try and implement new methods of farming and irrigation to help boost the agriculture sector by provision of loans and Kisan Credit Cards.

2

HEALTH IS WEALTH

"It is health that is real wealth and not pieces of gold and silver." – Mahatma Gandhi

The greatest wealth is our own health. A healthy body can earn great wealth but, a wealthy person cannot earn great health. We live in a fast moving world where individuals have no time for themselves. Most part of the life withers away in search of materialistic wealth in order to outshine others but, en route they lose their health. People eat junk foods and other unhealthy food items just for taste. They don't even have time to nourish their bodies with the required diet. A good and balanced diet reduces the stress level and promotes healthy life without any sufferings. Thus, it stands for utmost importance to individuals to analyse the significance of a healthy body.

A healthy diet is one that helps to maintain or improve overall health. We should consume a balanced diet consisting of essential nutrition: liquids, adequate proteins, essential fatty acids, vitamins, minerals, and calories. We must eat fresh fruits, salad, green leafy vegetables, milk, egg, yoghurt, etc. on time in order to maintain a healthy body. A healthy body also needs some daily physical activities, proper rest and sleep, cleanliness, healthy environment, fresh air and water, personal hygiene, etc. Also, we should drink more water at least 7-8 glasses of water. It balances blood pressure and supplies vital nutrients very fast to the body. A fit and healthy person becomes more resistant to infections and diseases.

Wealth matters however, not as important as health. Spending lots of money on junk food in five star hotels or on other entertainment sources like watching movie for a day etc. doesn't have any benefits other than self enjoyment. Being physically and mentally healthy helps a person to be socially and financially healthy too. A healthy person becomes more active, lively and energetic and works with full efficiency however; a rich but diseased person gets easily tired and eventually losses the wealth of lifetime i.e. health.

A healthy person can earn lots of money however an unhealthy person cannot because of the lack of motivation, interest and concentration level. Money is the source to live a healthy life however good health is the source to live a happy and peaceful life. So, everyone should take much precaution in maintaining a good health. Everyone should be away from bad habits and unhealthy life style. Being healthy is not only the state of being free of disease, illness or injury but also being happy physically, mentally, socially, intellectually and financially. Good health is actual necessity of happy life and the biggest blessing from the nature.

3

INCREDIBLE INDIA

India or Bharat (literally meaning, quest for knowledge) is the land of "Unity in diversity", a country that provides home to approximately 1.25 billion people with different mother tongues, belonging to different regions, castes and creeds. It is known as worldwide for its diversity of cultures, traditions, languages, food, clothing and spices. The country is the seventh largest in the world covering an area of approximately 3, 287,263 km and is the only one in the world having two official names, India and Bharat.

India is a sovereign, socialist, secular and democratic republic which is ruled by the people, made for the people and of the people. It consists of 29 states and 7 union territories with every state having its own bounty of rich cultural legacy. Religions like Hinduism, Christianity, Buddhism, Jainism, Sikhism, Islam, Judaism and Zoroastrianism are practiced by the people throughout the country. About 23 languages are recognised by the constitution of India as "Official languages", whereas numerous others are practiced throughout the nation.

India has a rich cultural heritage. From Kerala to Kanyakumari, the country is enriched with beautiful snow peaks, plateaus, valleys, water bodies and plains. Every state and city has its own significance, Kashmir is majorly known for its Pashmina wool and apples, Nagpur for its oranges, Agra for Taj Mahal (one of the seven wonders in the world), Punjab for its agricultural inputs, Bihar for its minerals, Meghalaya for its weather and seasonal extravagances, Bangalore, the Silicon valley of India for its contribution to the IT sector, Karnataka and Kerala for its silk. Also, the country is rich in historical buildings like the Red Fort, Fatehpur Sikri, Qutub Minar, India gate, Meenakshi Temple, Charminar, Jantar Mantar and Ajanta and Alora caves.

The country is a major exporter of engineering goods (19 percent of the total exports), chemical and pharmaceutical products (14 percent), gems and jewellery (14 percent), agricultural and allied products including sugarcane, wheat, rice, cereals, etc. (10 percent) and textiles and clothing (10 percent), making Indian economy the world's seventh-largest by nominal GDP and third-largest by purchasing power parity (PPP). It is one of the fastest growing and most populous democracies of the world.

Once Hu Shih, the Former Ambassador of China said to US that, "India conquered and dominated China culturally for 20 centuries without ever having to send a single soldier across her border." India has always maintained cordial relations with most nations all over the world. It also played a vital role during the Non Aligned Movement and soon became of the world's largest arms importer between 2007 and 2011. Now, the country has the third largest military in the world with 1.325 million active troops comprising of Indian Army, the Indian Navy, and the Indian Air Force and subsidiary organisations include the Strategic Forces Command and three paramilitary groups: the Assam Rifles, the Special Frontier Force, and the Indian Coast Guard.

There has been no more revolutionary contribution than the one which the Hindus (Indians) made when they invented zero. Lancelot Hogben, English Mathematician.

India is the motherland of Sanskrit language, the mother of almost all the languages around the globe, India is the country which has the highest number of engineers and doctors, various type of games and sports like Kabaddi, Chess, Polo with Hockey being the National sport of India making it the sport's most successful team in the Olympics as of 2012 are played. India has also played a major role in popularising cricket making it the most popular sport in India and Board of Control for Cricket in India (BCCI), is one of the sporting bodies."Jana Gana Mana" is the National Anthem and "Vande Matram" is the National song of the nation.

Diversity can also be felt by the varied climatic conditions across the nation. Four seasons namely, summer, winter, autumn and spring prevail throughout the year in most of the parts of the country. Also, India has a variety of cuisines that can be observed by the food habits of the people ranging from Mughlai to south Indian cuisine to Gujarati to Punjabi cuisine.

The unity in diversity of India is the essence of the nation where 1.25 billion people worship 33 crores deities and hail in the name of god; some Shiva, some Allah!, some Waheguru! And some Jesus.

<table><tr><td>**4**</td></tr></table>

SWACHH BHARAT ABHIYAN

Swachh Bharat Abhiyan is a cleanliness drive initiated by the government of India and commenced by the Honourable Prime Minister, Narendra Modi. It was introduced on the 145th birth anniversary of the father of our nation, Mahatma Gandhi on 2nd of October in 2014 at Rajghat, New Delhi as a visionary step to fulfil the dream of a clean India.

The campaign is also known as the Clean India Mission or Clean India drive or Swachh Bharat Campaign and is a benchmark campaign that aims at eradicating open defecation by 2019 by constructing 12 crore toilets in rural areas and making India, a dirt-free and beautiful country to live in. It includes the construction of latrines, promotion of sanitation programmes in rural areas, cleaning of streets, roads, converting insanitary toilets into pour flush toilets, changing the infrastructure, eradicating manual scavenging, complete disposal and reuse of solid and liquid wastes, bringing behavioural changes in people and motivating health practices to take the country ahead. It is one of the biggest drives ever and about 3 million government employees and school and college students of India participated in this event.

People litter everywhere on roads, bus stands and railway platforms and the industries discharge their wastes into water bodies. It harms the environment as non-biodegradable wastes produce poisonous gases and pollute the environment. In order to make our country clean, we must adopt eco-friendly measures like systematic disposal of industrial wastes, throwing of garbage in the dustbin installed by the government and households must pack bio-degradable and non-biodegradable wastes separately.

Numerous celebrities like Sachin Tendulkar, Priyanka Chopra, Baba Ramdev, Salman Khan, Anil Ambani and International organisations like World Bank have helped raise fund for sustaining the drive and make it a success. Famous personalities walked on streets with a broom in their hand as a way to motivate people about severity of the issue and fill in them the fervour to make their country clean and dirt-free. Also, various government officers swept the corridors of Rashtrapati Bhawan the very next day the campaign started.

As a result of the campaign between April 2014 and January 2015, 31.83 lakh toilets were built and Karnataka led all the other states in construction of toilets under the programme. Till August 2015, 80 lakh toilets have been constructed under the program. Also, the government of India aims at launching a countrywide real-time monitoring system for toilets constructed under the Swachh Bharat Abhiyan by creating awareness among the people through catchy and informative advertisements in both urban and rural India.

The government of India released a "Cleanliness Ranking" for 73 cities on 15th February 2016 as an af-ter effect of the campaign and only ten cities namely, Mysuru, Chandigarh, Tiruchirapalli, New Delhi Municipal Council, Visakhapatnam, Surat, Rajkot, Gangtok, Pim-prichinchwad and Greater Mumbai were found clean.

Cleanliness is next to godliness. Thus, together as one nation all citizens of nation must join hands in order to fulfil the dream of a clean and beautiful India. It will not only add value to the standard of living of the citizens but will also enhance the image of the country abroad and will create greater opportunities as a means to nurture the growth and development.

5

TELANGANA

Telangana, the twelfth largest and twelfth most populous state of India was formed on 2nd June 2014 with Hyderabad as its capital. It falls in the southern part of the country and covers an area of approximately 114,840 square kilometres. Till 1948, major part of Telangana was ruled over by the Nizam of Hyderabad. It was known as the Telugu-speaking region of the princely state of Hyderabad which dissolved into one big state, Andhra Pradesh in the year 1956.

The word 'Telangana' is derived from the Sanskrit word "Trilinga or Trilinga Desa" which means 'the country of three lingas'. In the ancient time, Telangana was ruled by several empires namely, the Satavahana dynasty (230 BCE to 220 CE), the Kakatiya Dynasty (1083–1323), the Musunuri Nayaks (1326–1356) the Delhi Sultanate, the Bahmani Sultanate (1347–1512),Qutub Shahi dynasty (1512–1687), Mughal Empire (1687–1724) and Asaf Jahi Dynasty (1724–1948).

The Nizam of Hyderabad didn't want to merge with Indian Union but to remain independent during independence but the Government of India captured Hyderabad State on 17th September 1948 after a military operation called Operation Polo. Telangana is situated on the Deccan Plateau and two major rivers Godavri and Krishna flow through it. There is hot and dry climate for major part of the year. It has three National Parks: Kasu Brahmananda Reddy National Park in Hyderabad district, and Mahavir Harina Vanasthali National Park and Mrugavani National Park in Ranga Reddy district.

The official languages of the state are Telugu and Urdu. Telangana has 10 districts, 42 revenue divisions, and 462 mandals. According to the census conducted in 2011, Telangana's literacy rate was 66.46% with male literacy and female literacy to be 74.95% and 57.92% respectively. The economy of Telangana is majorly driven by agriculture and farming with rice being the major food crop. Other important crops include cotton, sugarcane, mango and tobacco. The state is also growing in fields like biotechnology and information technology. Now, it is one of the top IT states in India consisting of 68 special economic zones (SEZ).

The Telangana state has won CNBC-TV18 most promising state of the year award for the year of 2015 and the Jury for the India Business Leader Awards (IBLA) had collectively chosen Telangana for the award. The state is well connected by structured transportation system through roadways, railways, airways with the Mahatma Gandhi Bus Station (M.G.B.S) in Hyderabad, which is one of the largest bus stands in Asia. Various monuments like Charminar, Golconda Fort, Qutb Shahi Tombs, Chowmahalla Palace,Falaknuma Palace, Birla Mandir and Bhongir Fort, Warangal Fort are the places of attraction for tourists in the state of Telangana.

6

TOURISM IN INDIA

India has a myriad of cultures, languages and traditions. Every state represents diversity in demographics and festivals. This is what makes our country a tourist's glee. The tourism industry in India plays an important role in the economy and is growing at a tremendous rate. It generated Rs. 8.31 lakh crore accounting to 6.3 percent of the nation's GDP in 2015 and generated 37.315 million jobs (8.7% of its total employment). It is found that according to the Travel and Tourism Competitiveness Report 2015, India was ranked 52nd out of 141 countries. The report also stated that India has fairly good air transport (ranked 35th), specifically given the country's level of development, and reasonable ground transport infrastructure (ranked 50th). The country has good ranks on natural and cultural resources background (ranked 12th).

People from all over the world are attracted to India for its beauty, its unity in diversity, its festivals, cultures and traditions. Andhra Pradesh is one the 'most preferred' tourist destinations in India according to a survey done by the Economic Times. The places like Tirupati, Srikurmam, Sri Kalahastishwara Temple, Thimmamma Marrimanu, Pulicat lake and Prakasam Barrage are major tourist attractions in the state of Andhra Pradesh.

Bihar attracts tourists to many places like Gaya, Patna, Kesariya and Sasaram, New Delhi, the country's capital has several monuments like Red Fort, Jantar Mantar, India Gate, Qutub Minar, Lotus Temple and Akshardham Temple for tourists attraction. Many places like Jaipur, Jodhpur, Jaisalmer and Udaipur in Rajasthan are known for their palaces and forts. Kerala is famous for places like Munnar, Trivandrum, Cochin and Kovalam for beaches and beautiful scenery. Jammu and Kashmir attract tourists from all over the world for places like Dal Lake, Ladakh, Srinagar Pahalgam, Gulmarg, Yeusmarg and Mughal Gardens. Meghalaya is famous for places like Umiam lake, Cherrapunji for its rainfall and scenic bounty, Shillong, Elephant Falls, Shadthum Falls, Weinia falls, Bishop Falls, Nohkalikai Falls, Langshiang Falls and Sweet Falls and Maharashtra for places like Ajanta Caves, Ellora Caves, Elephanta Caves and Chhatrapati Shivaji Terminus.

Indian government is constantly working towards boosting up all sectors of the economy through increased investment, provision of subsidies and implementation of suitable laws. Thus, in order to boost tourism industry, the Government of India has decided to implement a new visa policy, which allows the visitors to get hold of a visa on arrival at 16 designated international airports by obtaining an Electronic Travel Authorisation online before arrival. Therefore, people don't have to visit the visa centre or the Indian consulate.

Tourism has improved tremendously due to technological establishments in the industry since last few decades but it needs to be enhanced. Crimes like robbery, theft, harassment, rape still holds people back from visiting India and cleanliness is a major concern. People throw garbage everywhere on roads and make the places dirty. Thus, in order to overcome the problem proper dustbins must be installed at all places, washrooms must be installed, eco-friendly modes of transportation should be used and awareness drives must be held at places to create awareness about the cleanliness issue.

The Swachh Bharat Abhiyan initiated by Mr. Narendra Modi is one such cleanliness drive that aims at making India a clean, dirt-free and beautiful nation. Other schemes and programmes like Tourism Vision Document 2030, which defines the challenges faced by this sector and gives details about the 'Tourism vision 2030', Medical and Wellness Tourism Promotion Board: It is a Board that will provide leadership of the Government within a framework of prudent and effective measures, thereby enabling promotion and positioning of India as a competent and credible medical and wellness tourism destination and launch of Bi-Lingual Website of Ministry of Tourism.

7

AIDS

AIDS or Acquired Immune Deficiency Syndrome is one of the most deadly diseases for mankind. It is caused by infection with the Human Immunodeficiency Virus (HIV) and deliberately breaks down the immune system of the body by entering in the white blood cells and rupturing the reproductive processes of the body. The cure to this disease hasn't been found till date and it was observed in the year 2014 that the virus took about 1.2 million lives.

HIV is commonly spread via blood and semen through unprotected sex (both penetrative and oral), mother to child during pregnancy, delivery of pregnancy, hypodermic needles and blood transfusions. Basically, the transfer of bodily fluids from one body to the other in the above mentioned forms causes the HIV virus to spread. But, some body liquids like saliva and tears don't transmit this virus. The first symptoms are usually characterised by a brief period of illness and then the other symptoms including fever, lethargy, nausea, headache, rashes, etc. can be noticed after a period of six months.

AIDS was first found by the United States Centers for Disease Control and Prevention (CDC) in the year 1981 and HIV infection was recognized during the beginning of the decade. In 1986, India witnessed the first case of AIDS infection in the prostitutes of Chennai and Tamil Nadu. AIDS not only has a great impact on the body functioning of individuals but also on the society, where it became a source of discrimination. People infected with the virus are teased, discriminated and made fun off in the society.

AIDS cannot be cured but surely be diagnosed by ELISA test and Western Blotting test and be partially treated by use of some drugs. The treatment for the disease is recommended as soon as the diagnosis is made and without treatment, the average survival time after infection is 11 years.

So, in order to prevent people from the deadly disease, the government should create awareness about the disease, dentists should be restricted to use sterilized equipments, people should avoid tattoos, ear, nose piercing and use of common blades in barber's shop. People should also have monogamous sexual relationships.

8

BRAIN DRAIN

Brain drain is defined as the migration of highly trained, skilled and educated personnel from one country to the other for better remuneration and facilities provided by the employer. This term was initially used by the United Kingdom to describe the arrival of Indian scientists and engineers in the country post colonial period. It causes the origin country the loss of expertise and skills due to lack of opportunities and good pay scales.

Human emigration can be understood in three contexts namely, organisational, geographical and industrial. Organisational emigration refers to the migration of educated and skilled personnel from one organisation to the other, geographical emigration refers to the emigration of well qualified and trained individuals from their area of residence to other countries like United Kingdom or the United States for higher studies or jobs whereas industrial emigration is referred to as the movement of traditionally skilled workers from one sector of an industry to another. Movement of humans from one place to the other is basically in search of better job opportunities, higher standard of living and proper infrastructures. It sometimes leads to population explosion of the areas of movement.

Instances of human migration can be traced from the recent past. During the Holocaust in Europe, the country experienced influx of intelligentsia. Albert Einstein had immigrated permanently to the United States in the year 1933 and Sigmund Freud, Austrian neurologist and the founder of psychoanalysis, had finally decided to emigrate permanently with his wife and daughter to London, England, in 1938.

Brain drain has become a major area of concern in the developing countries like India leading to loss of skilled and qualified professionals like doctors, engineers, scientists and technicians. High cut-offs in the national universities, outdated courses and low pay scales add to the misery of the people. Students and professionals who are not able to get the required courses or packages tend to migrate to other countries.

Movement of Indian scientists, doctors and engineers to the United States has increased by 85% in last 10 years, a report of the chief scientific body of the United States outlined. And among all the Asian countries, India continued its trend of being the top country of birth for migrant scientists, doctors and engineers, with 9,50,000 out of Asia's total 2.96 million. India's 2013 report showed an 85% increase from 2003. From the year 2003 to 2013, the number of scientists, doctors and engineers dwelling in the US rose from 21.6 million to 29 million. As per the UNESCO report, 2009 China surpassed the figure of students going abroad by 421,000, following India with an approximate migration of 153, 300 students.

Vijay Raghavan, the secretary of the department of biotechnology rightly said, "India's huge population of talented youth means that we have enough young minds who can contribute to India from India and to India from outside India. We must continue to develop more excellent institutions and opportunities here so that the best talents have avenues here and not only abroad. This development of excellence is indeed required for the fast development of our country."

Our Prime Minister, Narendra Modi rightly said, 'We must reverse 'brain drain' into 'brain gain'. The government of India is working towards achieving the goal and has been successful in it too. The rate of brain drain has decreased in the recent past due to measures adopted by the government. Also, in order to curb the practice, the government and private institutions focus much on creating high scale job opportunities and better working environments. Also, universities must work on the cut-offs lists and aim at providing quality education to all potential individuals.

9

CHILD LABOUR

According to The Child Labour (Prohibition and Regulation) Act of 1986, it is prohibited to employ children below the age of 14 years in hazardous occupations identified in a list by the law. Indian law has listed 64 industries in the category.

Child labour is the practice to employ children less than 14 years of age at work. It not only deprives them of their childhood but also hinders their mental and physical growth. Children are meant to learn, not to earn. One can glance a lot of small children working at tea stalls, restaurants and other hazardous industries. They are exploited at work. They are not even provided with safe environment to work in. Even then, it is shocking to note that, India has the highest population of child labour of about 4.98 million. The unorganised agriculture sector employs about 60 percent of the child labour population and the organised sector (manufacturing, packaging, hunting, transportation, etc.) employs approximately 40 percent of the remaining population.

Illiteracy, poverty, superstitious beliefs, improper healthcare and educational facilities are major causes of child labour in India. Child labour predates to the colonial era, where children were used as bonded labour and trafficked to several areas to get work done at lower costs. Parents too could not help their children break free from the clutches due to indebtedness towards the landlords as they were further exploited by the middlemen to the core. Children work as farmers, plantation workers, maids, etc. According to 2005 the Government of India NSSO (National Sample Survey Organization), child labour occurrence rates in India is maximum among Muslim

Indians, about 40% higher than Hindu Indians and tribal populations of about 4 percent. Indian law allows children to work with their family in family based trades/occupations, for the purpose of learning a new trade/craftsmanship or vocation. But the industries take the advantage of child labour by providing lower wages for the same work and parents too are forced to engage their children to get money home. Not only India, other countries like Africa, Australia, Switzerland and Brazil collectively contribute to about 217 million children employed as labour, some even as full-time workers.

Many NGOs like Bachpan Bachao Andolan, Child Fund, CARE India, Talaash Association, Child Rights and You, Global March Against Child Labour, RIDE India, Childline etc. have been working to eradicate child labour in India. Also, in 2013, a major benchmark in the name of child labour was given by the Punjab and Haryana court directing to the total ban on the employment of children less than 14 years of age. Indian government guarantees punishment against child labour incidences in a number of acts including The Factories Act of 1948, The Mines Act of 1952, The Juvenile Justice (Care and Protection) of Children Act of 2000 and The Right of Children to Free and Compulsory Education Act of 2009.

Indian government and various international bodies like International Labour Organization (ILO) and National Child Labor Committee have taken several initiatives in order to prevent child labour throughout the world. But, the number has declined tremendously during the past few decades. These organisations have helped the number by working on the factors like reduction in poverty levels, changing the mindset of people, provision of the educational and healthcare facilities to the needy.

Child labour is a curse to the society. Many laws and programmes have been initiated by the government of India to control the incidences of child labour but unfortunately it still prevails. Making laws isn't enough, their implementation must be observed and checked with due creation of awareness about the serious problem of child labour.

10

CORRUPTION

Corruption is defined as the unethical conduct pursued by an individual confided with an authority or position. It can be seen everywhere today starting from the mixing of water in milk done by the milkmen to the bribe given by us to the government officials to get our work done. Also, it adversely affects the working of the economy and leads to stagnation. It starts from us and we are the ones who can weed out the cancer of corruption from our nation.

In 2015, India was ranked 76th out of 175 countries in Transparency International's Corruption Perceptions Index as compared to the neighbouring countries like Bhutan (30th), Nepal (126th), Bangladesh (145th), Sri Lanka (85th), etc. Many surveys have also been conducted in order to swot up the level of corruption in India. One survey says that more than 62 percent of Indians were found to have firsthand experience of paying bribes or influence peddling (use of power or influence to get the work done) to get jobs in public sector.

Corruption has spread its wings to other sectors of the economy as well. Public sector no more remains the only quintessence of it. Educational to health to NGOs, corporate to political sector, corruption squats everywhere. It breeds in almost every section of the society. It is the outcome of various disconcerting factors like bribery, tax invasion, red tapism, nepotism, monopolistic rule, etc. In 2011, a report prepared by KPMG noted that the key reasons for the prevalence of corruption in India are excessive regulation on bureaucracy and high tax bars.

The famous CWG Scam, 2G scam, Bofors scam, Abhishek Verma arms deals scam and Satyam scam are examples of the most prominent scandals that have stained the walls of Indian bureaucracy. There is an incessant list that accounts for a loss of more than billions of rupees caused by these scams to the nation.

Political corruption is subject to policy makers, bureaucrats and administrators of the nation. It occurs when they involve themselves in illegal practices like taking bribes and rewards for personal benefit at the expense of the nation as a whole.

Corporate corruption crops up as a means to benefit oneself at the expense of shareholders, used by corporate houses. It usually occurs in the relationships between the corporate houses and the suppliers or dealers.

Petty corruption deals with the involvement of payment of relatively small amounts of money to aid transactions like customs clearance or issuing of licences, etc.

Today, unscrupulous practices even prevail in the educational and health sector in the form of donations and bribery to the doctors, etc. Corruption in the health sector could mean the difference between the life and death of an individual whereas, the same in education sector would mean playing with the growth and developmental aspects of the economy.

Corruption destabilizes the economic development, political stability and government authenticity. It jeopardises the allocation of resources to the crucial sectors of the economy. The funds siphoned to many of the sectors don't reach the needy; they are consumed by the ministers and other government officials and transferred to their Swiss bank accounts. Also, it worsens the image of the nation in the international market.

Thus, it is now the responsibility of the citizens of the nation to carry out just and fair practices and cover up the loopholes in the administration and execution of laws if any. The government has also taken due measures in order to root out corruption from the nation. It has initiated various regulatory bodies and schemes to keep a check on the corruption statistics in India. Notable examples are the Right to Information act, Juvenile act, free and fair trails due to the enunciation of Fast track courts, PPP (Public Private Partnerships), e- ration cards, e- passports, etc. Media is yet another prominent element that has helped in decreasing the level of corruption by bringing out the naked truth behind corrupt individuals and organisations.

Therefore, we as citizens of the nation must take an oath to root out corruption from our nation and lead to better tomorrow as it starts from us and we are ones who can curb it. Reduction in the level of corruption will not only lead to a better administration system, a developed economy but all together a better world to live in.

11

FEMALE FOETICIDE

Female foeticide is still in practice in India from the time of advent of technological advancements in medical field like prenatal sex determination in the 1990s. However, earlier to this, female child was killed after the birth in many regions of the country. In the Indian society, female children are considered as social and economic burden to their parents; so they understand that it is better to kill them before birth. No one understands its negative aspects in the future. The female sex ratio in comparison to the males is reduced to a great extent (8 males per one female). It is not easy to compensate the sex ratio even if we stop female foeticide completely in the next few years.

With the development of ultrasound technique sex determination tests were made in the early 1990's. The couple in the Indian society continue to plan a child until they get baby boy killing all baby girls born earlier to the baby boy. In order to control the population and stop female foeticide, the Government of India has made various rules and regulations against female foeticide and trend of abortions after sex determination tests. Killing of a baby girl through abortion has been an offence all through the country.

Female foeticides have been in practice for centuries especially for the families who prefer only male child. There are various religious, social, financial and emotional reasons behind the killing of female child. Time has changed now to a great extent but this tendency of killing daughter is still prevalent in India.

Some key reasons of female foeticide are:

Generally, parents avoid baby girl because they have

35

to pay a big amount (more than their strength) as a dowry at daughter's marriage. There is a belief that girls are always consumer and boys are producer. Parents understand that a son earns money for them whole life and care their parents however girls will get married a day and go away. There is a myth that son will carry the name of family in future whereas girls have to carry husband's family. Parents and grandparents feel proud while having a baby boy in the family whereas the shame having daughter. There is a pressure on new bride of the family to give birth to a male child; thus she is forced to go for sex determination and abortion if the baby is girl. Daughters are given less respect and priority than sons in the Indian society from ancient time. They did not have same access like boys in the areas of education, healthcare, nutrition, play, etc. In order to combat with sex-selective abortions, there should be high level awareness among common public. Satyamev Jayate, a most famous programme run by the Aamir Khan on TV has done great to raise awareness among common public through its first episode of "Daughters Are Precious". Cultural interventions regarding this issue are needed to be addressed through awareness programmes. Recent awareness programmes like *Beti Bachao Beti Padhao*, or *Save girls campaign*, etc. have been made regarding girl's rights.

Female infanticide or female feticide is mainly because of the sex determination. There should be legal step to get control over it. Every citizen of India must abide by the law. And one should be surely punished if found guilty for this cruel practice. Licences of hospitals must be cancelled permanently and doctors should be punished if found guilty. Marketing of medical equipments especially for illegal sex determination and abortion should be stopped. Parents should be penalized, who want to kill their baby girl. Campaigns and seminars should be regularly organized to aware young couples. Women should be empowered so that they can be more attentive to their rights.

12
GENDER DISCRIMINATION

Gender discrimination is defined as unequal treatment on the basis of gender or sex, which leads to disparate opportunities. In India, girls and women are majorly affected by many social evils which shows disparities in educational qualifications, political influence, employment opportunities, salaries and wages, etc. They are perceived to be disadvantaged both at work and home. It has prevailed in the Indian subcontinent since ages and people are still suffering from it although the Constitution of India has granted equal rights for both men and women. Every individual has the right to be treated equally on the basis of gender, caste, creed and religion as per the fundamental human rights mentioned in the constitution.

Female infanticide and sex-selective abortion is practiced in India and majorly reflects the low status of Indian women. Census 2011 witnessed a sharp decline in the girl population (as a percentage to total population) under the age of seven and the 2005 census showed that the infant mortality estimates for females and males are 61 and 56, respectively, out of 1000 live births, with girls more likely to be aborted than boys due to biased behavioural patterns among people. Sons are preferred over daughters as they are thought to become heirs of the ancestral property and take the name ahead. Even wealthy and literate families followed the practice.

Education is yet another parameter of gender inequality that prevails in India. Most of the parents don't send their daughters for higher education since they believe that they are only meant for household chores and investing in their career or education would not pay them anything in return. Literacy for females stands at 65.46%, compared to 82.14% for males. Expected years of schooling for women is 11.3 and for men is 11.8 approximately and the ratio to males in primary and secondary education is 0.98 - 1.0

Not only this, considering the aspect of female employment opportunities, they are unfairly paid in comparison to males for the same work. According to a research, Indian women earn 64% of what their male counterparts earn for the same occupation and the level of qualification on an average. During 2005-06, Work-force Participation Rate of women was about 31% in rural areas and 14% in urban areas. On the other hand, for males, the WPR was about 56% both in rural areas and in urban areas. Also, the discrimination is majorly seen in the health sector as well, the process of child-bearing exposes women to specific health care and associated risks. As per the SRS based researches, MMR had declined from 301 per one lakh live births to 254 per one lakh live births during 2004–06.

The government of India has taken various initiatives in order to empower women and grant them equal status as men. Enactment of laws like Criminal Amendment Act, 2013, the Protection of Women from Domestic Violence Act, 2005; Dowry Prohibition Act, 1961;Indecent Representation of Women (Prohibition) Act, 1986; the Sexual Harassment of Women at Workplace (Prevention, Prohibition and Redressal) Act, 2013, the Prohibition of Child Marriage Act, 2006 (PCMA), Equal Remuneration Act, 1976, Maternity Benefit Act, 1961 and 73rd – 74th Amendment of the Constitution mandating 33% reservation for women in the local governance are a few examples. It also organises campaigns for creating awareness about the problem and for educating parents about the issue.

Gender equality will only be reached if we are able to empower men, Michelle Bachelet

Women and girls have always been considered as a liability to the family, they are only meant to do the household chores and support raising of children. The Age specific mortality rate (ASMR) in year 2000 was observed to be 8.9 and has come down to 6.8 in the year 2008. But, today the scenario has changed, women support their families financially as well. Girls have surpassed boys in a lot of fields ranging from education to employment. Thus, there is an underlying need for the parents and Indian society as a whole to understand the need of equality on the basis in order to have their daughters like Kalpana Chawla, Kiran Bedi, Indra Nooyi etc. much competent to sons.

13

NOISE POLLUTION

Noise pollution is defined by the activities that harm human or animal life due to unwanted disturbances caused by noise elements like machines and transportation systems, motor vehicles, aircraft, trains and outdoor noise including environmental noises. Noise refers to unwanted sound and has adverse effects on people and the environment. Sound becomes unwanted when it either hampers day to day activities like sleeping, conversation, or ebbs the quality of life.

Noise pollution can lead to both health and behavioural problems such as hypertension, cardiovascular diseases, coronary artery disease, increased blood pressure, high stress levels and hearing problems in humans. Symptoms of noise-instigated stress include sudden losses of temper, irritability, depression, aggression, hostility, and argumentative behaviour. Also, it has pernicious effects on the existence of wildlife, for example, Zebra finches become less faithful to their partners when exposed to traffic noise. It leads to reduction in usable habitat, hearing problems, etc.

Until the 1970s governments all over the world didn't consider noise as an environmental threat. But, later it was considered as a threat to human health and precautionary measures were taken to reduce noise pollution and create awareness. International Noise Awareness Day is a worldwide campaign which was sun in 1996 by the Center of Hearing and Communication (CHC), intended to raise awareness about the impact of noise on the welfare and health of people. Also, the government of India has enforced rules and regulations against firecrackers and loudspeakers, but enforcement is awfully slack. Awaaz (sound) Foundation is yet another initiative taken by Indian government. It is an NGO functioning to control noise pollution from various sources through advocacy, public interest litigation, awareness, and educational campaigns since 2003.

Noise pollution has adverse effects on the wellbeing of mankind and animal life. Therefore, we must take required steps in order to minimise noise pollution to maintain ecological system.

In order to reduce noise, we must limit heavy vehicles on road, use quieter jet engines, and redesign industrial equipments to make them eco-friendly. Quiet programs and initiatives have been taken up as an attempt to reduce occupational noise exposures. These programs encourage the purchase of quieter tools and equipment and persuade manufacturers to design quieter equipment as precautionary measure.

14

POPULATION EXPLOSION

Population explosion refers to a huge and drastic increase in the number of people residing in a particular area or region. It is conceived as one of the greatest threats to the development and growth of the economy. Between 1959 and 2000, the world's population increased from 2.5 billion to 6.1 billion and according to United Nations extrapolations, the world population will rise between 7.9 billion and 10.9 billion by the year 2050. The World population has significantly risen only after the 1700s.

The developed countries like U.S.A. and United Kingdom comprises limited population with ample amount of resources in hand. They are rich enough to employ all potential individuals according to their skills leading to growth and development prospects of the nation as a whole whereas, underdeveloped nations like Gambia, Liberia and developing nations like India and China are the worst hit by the problem of population explosion. The number of job opportunities created in the country is not even equal to half of the population. India is anticipated to be the world's most populous country by 2022, exceeding China. Today India accounts for 15% of the world population consisting of 1.25 billion people approximately, whereas the land area comprises only 2.4% and according to 1981 census, the population in India was 685 million including about 354 million males and 331 million females.

Population explosion is majorly due to many factors like increased birth rate, decreased infant mortality rate, improved life expectancy and ignorance about family planning. It has a widespread impact on the economic and social stability of the economy leading to problems like overpopulation, increase in the level of poverty, illiteracy, unemployment, increasing health problems, increasing environmental problems like pollution and global warming due to extra pressure on the earth than it can handle, etc.

Population Connection formerly known as Zero Population Growth or ZPG is a non-profit organization in the United States which aims at raising awareness about the population challenges and exponents for enhanced global access to family planning and reproductive health care. Many organisations all around the globe are working in order to control the menace caused by the problem. The government of India both at central and state levels have implemented laws and policies in order to curb the problem. The Family Planning is an official programme launched in 1952 that aims at acknowledging people about the importance of family planning. The parents were convinced to go in for sterilization after the birth of two children as contraceptive pills were not always found to be safe and full-proof. The state governments too came forward to help the central government in its bid to attain success in population control. Cheap contraceptives were distributed in even the remotest villages, sex education was popularized, vasectomy operations were conducted and abortion was legalized. Also, the government is trying to educate the people by initiating RTE (Right To Education) Act that guarantees free and compulsory education for children between 6 and 14 in India under Article 21A of the Indian Constitution.

Thus, in order to control the situation we must also seek to control the birth rate and do family planning. This in turn will not only better our lives but will also better the nation as a whole. The activities of the nation in independent India are directed towards the task of providing adequate means of livelihood to an increasing number of people through an incorporated development of all sectors ranging from agriculture to trade to commerce and industries. The schemes adopted and implemented for this purpose cannot materialize unless the population problem is tackled satisfactorily.

15

REGIONALISM: A NEW KIND OF TERRORISM

Regionalism is an ideology and political movement that seeks to advance the causes of a region. As a process it plays a significant role within the nation as well as outside the nation i.e. at international level. Regionalism has positive as well as negative impact on society, polity, diplomacy, economy, security, culture, development, negotiation, etc.

If the interest of one region or a state is asserted against the country as a whole or against another region/state in a hostile way, and if a conflict is promoted by such alleged interests, then it can be called as regionalism.

Roots of regionalism lie regionalism in India's manifold diversity of languages, cultures, ethnic groups, communities, religions and so on, and is encouraged by regional concentration of those identity markers, and fuelled by a sense of regional deprivation. For many centuries, India remained the land of many regions, cultures and traditions.

For instance, southern India (the home of Dravidian cultures), which is itself a region of many regions, is evidently different from the north, the west, the central and the north-east. Even the East of India is different from the North-East of India comprising seven constituent units of Indian federation today with the largest concentration of tribal people.

Regionalism has remained perhaps the most potent force in Indian politics ever since independence (1947). It has remained the basis of many regional political parties which have governed many states since the late 1960s. Three clear patterns can be identified in the post-independence phases of accommodation of regional identity through statehood.

First, in the 1950s and 1960s, intense (ethnic) mass mobilisation, often taking on a violent character, was the main force behind the state's response with an institutional package for statehood. Andhra Pradesh in India's south showed the same pattern. The fast unto death in 1952 of the legendary (Telugu) leader Potti Sriramulu for a state for the Telegu speakers out of the composite Madras Presidency moved the leader Jawaharlal Nehru, a top nationalist leader and it was followed by State reorganisation commission under Fazal Ali paving way for State Reorganization Act, 1956.

Second, in the 1970s and 1980s, the main focus of reorganization was India's North-east. The basis of reorganization was tribal insurgency for separation and statehood. The main institutional response of the Union government was the North-eastern States Reorganisation Act, 1971 which upgraded the Union Territories of Manipur and Tripura, and the Sub-State of Meghalaya to full statehood, and Mizoram and Arunachal Pradesh (then Tribal Districts) to Union Territories. The latter became states in 1986. Goa (based on Konkani language (8th Schedule)), which became a state in 1987, was the sole exception.

Third, the movements for the three new states — Chhattisgarh from Madhya Pradesh, Jharkhand from Bihar and Uttaranchal form Uttar Pradesh — were long-drawn but became vigorous in the 1990s. And the most recent example is the division of Andhra Pradesh, in a separate Telangana state, which started functioning in 1950s.

Regional economic inequality is a potent time bomb directed against national unity and political stability giving rise to terrorism. Regional diversification of languages and culture is a major factor that contributed to terrorism.

16

TERRORISM

"**S**eeing a man praying to Allah is enough for some people to assume he is a terrorist."– Damian Lewis

However, it is rightly said by Vladimir Putin that "Terrorism has no nationality or religion. Terrorism is referred to as the political, religious and ideological activities that make use of terror or violence in order to fulfil personal selfish motives. It is one of the most hazardous problems that the whole world is facing today. According to the US State Department, it majorly contains four elements. The first is an act of violence. The second is a political objective and the third is that threat of violence is a direct attack on civilians. Lastly, it is usually committed by a supporting nation or nations of terrorism.

Terrorist activities have a widespread impact on mankind. These activities generate fear and anxiety in the minds of the people making them subjective to the ideologies of attacking group by undermining the state rule. Also, it disrupts travel and tourism and wastes potential resources of the economy through terrorist attacks. People fear travelling to countries where these activities are carried out. It is also observed that over 3 lakh innocent people died due to terrorist attacks from 2006 to 2014. Initially 'terrorism' was referred to as the acts committed by a government but at present it is usually referred to as the killing of innocent people.

Terrorism takes various forms depending upon the country and its political system namely, civil disorder, political terrorism, non-political terrorism, criminal terrorism and official terrorism i.e. terrorism referring to those nations whose rule is based upon fear and oppression that is similar to terrorist activities. Terrorism can be carried out by individuals, groups and organisations. Aden-Abyan Islamic Army, Jaish-e-Mohammed, Al-Qaeda, ISIS and Lashkar-e-Taiba are some of the recognised terrorist organisations that are responsible for the violent activities that take place all around the globe. The attack on World Trade Center on September 11, 2001 was carried out by Al-Qaeda in United States. Other activities include the German bombing of London, the Japanese bombing of Pearl Harbour, the British fire bombing of Dresden, and the U.S. atomic bombing of Hiroshima during World War II.

Domestic terrorism prevails in democratic countries like India, United Kingdom, United States, Israel, Spain and Indonesia very much. In a democratic country the government is made by the people, for the people and of the people. Democratic nations provide equal rights and freedom to its citizens to participate in the entire decision making but in countries like Brunei, Qatar, Oman, Iran and Iraq where the country is ruled by monarchs the dictatorship prevails and the civilians have no freedom of expression. This results in anger against the state leading to terrorist activities done in order to undermine state or monarchical laws.

Religious terrorism finds its roots in nations where majority of communist groups undermine the other minority groups by doing violent activities. Terrorism doesn't takes place only between nations for fulfilling selfish motives but also, takes place internally within citizens and individuals. Intimate terrorism refers to the violent activities that are carried out by one intimate partner over the other for emotional gains or fulfilling ego. Violence by a person against their intimate partner is often done as a means to control their partner but it does not happen on frequent basis. Terrorist attacks are often targeted to increase fear and publicity, usually by utilising explosives or poison.

There is a lot of concern about terrorist attacks employing weapons of mass destruction.

Mass media performs the job of watchdogs of the democracy and scrutinise and analyse all the aspects regarding the welfare of the state. They have also been successful in minimising the extent of terrorism in various forms. The governments around the globe must take precautionary measures in order to minimise the activities. People who join these terrorist organisations and harm mankind in the name of religion and selfish motives need to be taught the real essence. Also, they must not be jailed and fed good food but they must be punished instead.

17

URBANISATION

"Urbanization is not about simply increasing the number of urban residents or expanding the area of cities. More importantly, it's about a complete change from rural to urban style in terms of industry structure, employment, living environment and social security." -Li Keqiang

Urbanisation is basically defined as the increase in the proportion of population in the urban areas which results in the development of cities and towns. It is also a process through which rural areas are transformed into urban areas. It can be seen in almost every part of the world where humans reside. It is a result of increasing industrialisation and implied employment in big cities and towns. Better standard of living and other factors like modernisation and better infrastructure attract rural people to the urban areas. People in rural areas are mostly dependent on agriculture for their income and other necessities which is further dependent on seasonal changes. Thus, for major part of the year the rural people are unemployed.

During the 20th century, only about 15% of the world population lived in cities and later it was found by the UN in the year 2007 that more than 50% of the world population were living in cities, for the first time in human history.

Urbanization is a two-way process because it includes not only movement from village to cities and change from agricultural occupation to business, trade, service and profession but it also involves change in the attitudes, beliefs, values and behaviour patterns of migrants. The process of urbanisation takes two forms: demographic and sociological. Demographical urbanisation is defined as growth in the proportion of urban population whereas sociological urbanisation refers to the behaviour, institutions and other materialistic things that are identified as urban and leads to changes in the standard of living of the people. Thus, urbanisation includes migration of people, occupational shift, and land use shift from agricultural to non agricultural, from rural to urban areas.

Urbanisation leads to population explosion, pressure on the environment, etc. in the urban areas. Rural people majorly migrate to urban areas in search of better health facilities, schools, employment and career opportunities because villages lack proper infrastructure and job opportunities. Thus, it is very important for the government to realise the worth of rural sector and develop it in every possible way. Proper hospitals, schools, colleges and industries must be built in the villages in order to foster employment opportunities leading to development and growth of backward areas.

18

WATER CONSERVATION AND MANAGEMENT IN INDIA

Water is essential for life on our planet. It is required for many things including growth of food, maintaining ourselves clean, power generation, to control fire and most importantly to stay alive. Water is a part of our daily life and we are heavily dependent on it. The conservation of water is very important and necessary to have a healthy and long-lasting life. Conserving the water is not difficult, it saves money, and it is beneficial to our future. We do not know if there is enough water for a more crowded world in the future. We must learn about the importance of water, and conserve the water to prevent future problems. Water conservation refers to the reduction in usage of water. It can also include the recycling of water for purposes like irrigation, cleaning, and even treatment for later use. That is the reason why we need to conserve our water, in this case the Rio Grande water; it may be helpful for our future and might be used for other purposes.

Small changes such as not leaving the faucet running while brushing your teeth, or checking for leaks more often can make a big difference. All of these are very important.

Nowadays we use much more water than we ever did. Every human being uses hundreds of gallons of water per day. This makes a state's population use millions of gallons of water a day. All this consumption of water comes to a high cost, sometimes paying hundreds of dollars per month.

Reducing the water you use will save you money. Even though, water makes up about seventy percent of the earth's surface, only a small percentage of that water is good for human use. Reducing the amount of water used will help you economically and benefit you and coming generation in the future as well.

Water is the first necessity for survival on the earth. As we can see, the world's population is growing at a fast rate. We must take precautions for a sustainable fortune wherein people are well-equiped with at least the basic necessity of life i.e. water.

According to the survey by the National Crime Records Bureau recently, it has been recorded that around 16,632 farmers (2,369 women) finished their lives through suicide, however, 14.4% cases were because of drought. So, we can say that water scarcity is also the reason of illiteracy, suicide, fights and other social issues in India and other developing countries. In such regions of water scarcity, the children of new generation are not achieving their basic right to education and right to live happily.

Therefore, as responsible citizens of India, we should make ourselves aware about all the problems of water scarcity so that we all may take a pledge and join hands together for water conservation. There is a true saying that a small effort of everyone can give a big result just like many drops of water form a huge water body like pond, river and sea. We do not need to make extra efforts for water conservation, we only need to bring some positive changes in our daily activities, closing of the tap after every use tightly, use of bucket and mug while washing anything or bathing instead of using shower or pipe. A little effort from the end of millions of people can give a big and positive result towards the Save Water campaign.

19

A RIVER IN FLOOD

Floods are natural phenomena. They occur when there is heavy rain and the discharge of water is greater than the capacity of river channeled. Sometimes, it has been seen that due to fast melting of snow on the hill tops, the excess water begins to flow over the river banks and submerges the adjacent areas.

In our country, most of the floods are seasonal. They occur during the monsoon period which extends from June to September. Sometimes, there are torrential rains during this period and cause wide spread floods. The most flood prone basins are those of the Ganga in the northern plains of the Brahmaputra in Assam and the deltas of the Mahanadi, Godavari, Krishna and the Kaveri. The Brahmaputra has flooded more often and with greater severity in recent years.

One of the worst floods in more than fifty years to have hit India's eastern state of Assam caused massive destruction, displacement, disease and a mounting death toll. Last year the monsoon rains were heavy and torrential and they continued till September. As a result there occurred heavy loss of life and material. Many people did their best to help the affected families. Some private organisations also helped the needy.

The Government too came forward to assist them. Some private doctors were also called to give first aid on the spot. The affected whose condition was serious were removed to the hospitals in the Government ambulance car. There was acute scarcity of food stuff and drinking water in the affected areas. Hence, army and navy personnel mounted rescue operations. They dropped food packets and drinking water bottles from aeroplanes. In this way, every possible help was given to the flood victims

UNICEF also gave monetary help to the affected people of the state. Inspite of all these helps, there were still millions of people who had no place left to live in. Their homes and huts were washed away by the flood and they were forced to stay in refugee camps.

Of all forms of natural phenomena flooding is the most destructive and this leaves a trail of woes and suffering for mankind. They have the most damaging effect on the crops and livestock. In addition, the transport and communication links are also damaged. Many railway lines and roads are simply washed away by the fury of floods. Even after the swollen river recedes, people became prey to many water borne diseases. There is always a fear of the outbreak of epidemics. Thus, floods have far reaching effects.

Floods can be controlled by adopting the following measures:

1. Construction of embankents, flood walls and ring bunds.

2. Construction of flood control reservoirs which can temporarily hold a part of flood within the storage space provided in the reservoir so that the rate of flow below the reservoir is kept within safe limits.

3. Improvement of surface drainage.

4. Reducing the rate of runoff by watershed management.

5. Construction of raised platform to be used during times of flood emergency.

6. Afforestation of the catchment areas of the rivers.

7. Building of storage dams across those small streams, which have devastated large areas in the past.

8. Straightening of the meandering river channels.

9. Establishment of proper flood warning systems.

Man has got great achievements in the field of science technology. He has conquered over the nature in various ways but not completely. He is still helpless in the face of natural furies because he is not able to develop a technique to control them.

20

OUR UNIVERSE

Universe means unimaginably vast space which is unbounded with its dots. The universe includes everything that abounds in space, and space is filled with matter which varies from the tiniest and cosmic particle to the gigantic galaxies. The universe is known to be composed of many types of comparatively small and large bodies e.g., the galaxies, the constellations (star groups), the stars, the planets and other heavenly bodies.

Scientists believe that the universe was created due to a massive explosion called the 'big bang'. A long time after the big bang, stars like our sun were formed. At that time, clouds of hot gases and particles revolved around the sun. Over the time, many particles got stuck together to form large bodies. These bodies pulled smaller objects towards them by gravitational force. This made them larger still. These bodies finally became the planets.

Astronomers have found that the universe consists of galaxies, black holes, comets, planets, satellites. Stars contribute to the formation of galaxies and black holes. Galaxies are clusters of millions or trillions of stars having mass trillion times the mass of our sun. Galaxies have different shapes like spiral, elliptical, irregular. Our galaxy is the Milky Way and is spiral in shape. The Sun is one of the 100 million stars in the Milky Way. From this, we can imagine the vastness of the milky way and universe.

A galaxy is a rotating stellar system (star system) consisting of a swarm of stars which are held together by gravitational force. In other words, a galaxy is an enormously large cluster of stars. Our galaxy to which the sun along with its planet families belong is an aggregate of about one hundred billion stars. Ours is called "Milky way" galaxy which looks like a discus (a disc-shaped metal used in discus throw) when viewed through powerful optical telescope. A group of stars which seem to form a pattern is called a constellation.

All stars are huge balls of hydrogen and helium gases. In a star, hydrogen gets converted into helium. In this reaction, a large amount of energy is liberated. This is the source of the heat and light of a star. Stars vary in brightness and size. Some are medium-sized, like our sun. Some are so huge that if they were to be placed in our sun's position, they would fill the entire solar system.

The sun is the brightest object in the sky. It is huge. It is about 333,000 times heavier than the earth, and you can fit more than a million earths inside it. Its great mass causes a large gravitational force. This keeps the sun, the planets, their moon and some other smaller bodies together as the family of the sun. The sun and all the bodies moving around sun are together called solar system. All the members of the solar system revolve around the sun in almost circular paths or in orbits.

Planets and satellites are non-luminous heavenly bodies which shine only because of reflection of star (sun) light from their surface. The planets whirl round their stars in definite orbits. There are Eight planets in our solar system namely Mercury, Venus, Earth, Mars, Jupiter, Saturn, Uranus, and Neptune, Mercury being the closest and Neptune being the farthest from the sun.

A dwarf planet is a small, round body that orbits the sun. At the time of its formation, a dwarf planet can not pull all other objects towards its orbit. So it is not considered as a planet. Pluto, which was previously considered a planet, is now considered a dwarf planet. Ceres and Eris are two other dwarf planets.

In a belt between the orbits of Mars and Jupiter, millions of small, irregular, rocky bodies revolve around the sun. These are asteroids, and the belt is known as the asteroid belt. Asteroids are also called minor planets. As they enter the earth's atmosphere, they heat up because of friction with the air, and start burning. As these burning meteoroids fall towards the ground, they are seen as streaks of light on the earth. The streak of light caused by a burning meteoroid is called a meteor or a shooting star.

A comet is a small body of ice and dust that moves around the sun in an elongated orbit. As a comet approaches the sun, it heats up and leaves behind a stream of hot, glowing gases and dust particles. We see this gas as the 'tail' of the comet. Thus, our universe is made up of several large and small bodies connected with each other through the force of attraction.

21

OZONE LAYER DEPLETION

Ozone layer is a protective shield that exists in the earth's stratosphere (layer above the troposphere where aircrafts fly) and absorbs sun's ultraviolet rays. It saves earth from the ultraviolet rays falling directly on the surface of the earth. The ozone layer absorbs about 97–99 percent of the Sun's ultraviolet radiations which would otherwise cause a lot of damage to all life forms near the earth's surface. The layer contains major proportion of ozone gas (O_3) which is formed in the stratosphere when ultraviolet rays strikes oxygen molecule.

Ozone layer is depleting at a fast pace since the past few decades due to OCDs (Ozone depleting sources) like CFCs (Chlorofluorocarbons), halons, methyl bromide, methyl chloroform, carbon tetrachloride and trichloroethane. OCDs are stubborn substances that stay in the earth's atmosphere even after rains and get transported to the stratosphere, which causes depletion of the ozone layer. It leads to numerous biological consequences such as increase in sunburn, skin cancer, cataracts, damage to plants, and reduction in population of aquatic animals in the oceans. CFCs are a by-product of human manufactures. They are used as packaging materials, aerosol spray cans and cooling units in refrigerators and air conditioners. These are also used as disinfectants and bleaching agents and expected to be released up to a level of 5000 tonnes every year in India.

Polar Regions, Mid-latitude areas including Australia and Antarctica are some of the areas where the ozone layer is depleting at a very fast rate. It is believed that not only human causes but also volcanic eruptions lead to thinning of the ozone layer. Therefore, countries like America, India, Canada, Sweden, Denmark, and Norway are working to eliminate the use of CFCs in aerosol spray cans, air conditioners and refrigerators. Due to the initiatives taken by these countries. The Intergovernmental Panel on Climate Change (IPCC) report review of ozone observations and model calculations concluded that global amount of ozone has now been approximately stabilized.

Also, the Montreal Protocol of the United Nations Environment Programme 1989 on Substances that Deplete the Ozone Layer (a protocol to the Vienna Convention for the Protection of the Ozone Layer) is an international treaty devised to protect the ozone layer by eliminating the production of numerous substances that are responsible for ozone depletion including the OCDs.

22

AGRICULTURE – THE SOUL OF INDIAN ECONOMY

"India lives in villages and agriculture is the soul of Indian economy", said Mahatma Gandhi.

The statement stands true till date. India is a fast growing economy with agriculture playing a vital role in it. In spite of developments in the service and industrial sector, agriculture being the primary sector has always been the mainstay of Indian economy. As per statistics of 2015-16, agriculture and allied sector (including livestock, forestry and fishery) are the largest contributor to the GDP (Gross Domestic Product) with a share of 10 percent of total exports in India.

About 70 percent of the Indian population resides in the rural areas. Agriculture being their main occupation provides them with their key source of income. Over 58% of the households in India depend on agriculture as their principal means of livelihood. Agriculture meets the food requirements of our people and ensures food security for the country. Production of food grains and non food grains has made India self sufficient. It has majorly added on to the national income of our country. Several other industries are also dependant on agriculture for their supplies as it produces several raw materials for them. It lays a foundation of several major industries like textile, sugar mill, oil etc. Other industries such as tractor manufacturing, pesticides, fertilizers etc. are also dependant on agriculture.

Indian agriculture predates to the Rigveda, when agriculture started as a result of early cultivation of plants and crops and domestication of animals. Since beginning the man has been trying to find out new methods and tools for farming. Due to the constant efforts made by the man, he found out new agricultural techniques to improve production and quality of food stuffs. In the middle ages and modern era, the irrigation channels helped agriculture reach a new level. Later during the Colonial British era, Indian agriculture made its mark in the global market. After independence, the Republic of India saw special programs introduced to focus on the improvement of food and cash crop supply.

India with its rich soils, ample sunshine, sufficient water resources and diverse climatic conditions is suitable for growing various types of crops. It has the highest percentage of land under cultivation in the world. In spite of this fact, the productivity of agriculture is fairly low. Our agriculture is in a bad condition which is a matter of great concern. Thus, improvements in the state of agriculture are of extreme importance for the progress of our country. In the present scenario, the challenges in our agricultural sector are quite different from those in the previous decade. There is an enormous amount of pressure to produce more food with shrinking natural resources. In order to keep the momentum of growth, a careful economic evaluation is required.

India has shown steady yet significant boost in the agricultural sector over the past 60 years. This transformation in the sector is the outcome of India's Green Revolution. It was introduced in India in late 1960s. It offered improved agricultural technologies to overcome the low production problems in India. It also introduced hybrid seeds which are higher-yielding varieties (HYVs) of seeds, and increased the use of fertilizers, and applied irrigation methods and modern farming techniques. This in turn boosted the production manifolds required to make India self sufficient, thus improving the state of agriculture in India. To improve the agricultural condition of our country and to boost economic growth the Indian government introduced Five year plans. The first Five-year mainly focused on primary sector and was a big success and so where the subsequent ones. As the Five year plans accorded priority to the agricultural sector, in the past 50 years the food grain production in India has increased substantially from 51 million tonnes in 1950-51 to 253.16 million tonnes in the year 2014-15. Also our agricultural universities are working as a role model for other developing nations.

Indian agriculture meets the food requirement of not only our own country, but also several other countries of the world. Hence, with appropriate measures, introduction and implementation of new techniques and optimum utilization of our resources, the agricultural sector in India can be boosted and brought to a new level, which in turn will add on to the overall economic development of India. Farmers should be encouraged to indulge in mixed farming techniques and consolidation of fragmented land. Micro-irrigation should be taken up by the farmers to reduce cost of production. It streams irrigation which helps in conserving water. It also reduces fertilizer inputs and ensures higher productivity.

23

INDIAN ECONOMY

India is an agro-based economy but lot of emphasis has been given on the development of industries, service sector (including construction, trade, commerce, banking system etc.) and socio-economic infrastructure (like education, health, housing power, energy, transport, communication etc.). Indian economy can be broadly divided into two heads Public Sector and Private Sector.

Public Sector: It consists of all the economic organizations which are controlled and managed by the government. All the government-owned production units come under this head. These units produce and distribute goods and services among the common mass with an objective of welfare motives.

Private Sector: It consists of all the economic enterprises which are controlled and managed by the private enterprises. All the privately owned production units are come under this head. These units produce and distribute goods and services among the people with an objective of profit motive.

When the Britishers left, our country was economically backward. The self-sufficient village economy based on cottage industries and old handicraft items were losing demand because of the introduction of new industrial products.

With the decline of cottage and handicraft industries, the traditional economic base of Indian society was in bad shape. On the other hand, there was insufficiency in the field of industrial society as well. As a consequence majority of the population in our country remained undeveloped and poverty-stricken.

At the time of Independence, the economy of our country was poor. The Indian Government had to plan for balanced economic growth and development of the country. The eradication of poverty, illiteracy and industrial and technological underdevelopment were the most important challenges before the country.

The Constitution in the chapter Directive Principles of State Policy laid down the methods for securing economic development and economic justice. The state shall direct its policy towards securing the following: Providing adequate means of livelihood; Distributing the ownership of material resources of the community for common good; The prevention of concentration of wealth; securing equal pay for equal work for both men and women; securing of all the workers reasonable wages and a decent standard of life; raise the standard of living and to improve public health; state shall try to promote cottage industries.

The Government of India has undertaken several initiatives aiming at economic growth and development. For the industrial and technological development of the country, our Constitution provides for setting up of a Planning Commission now transformed into National Institution for Transforming India (NITI Aayog) to frame plans and programs for the rapid economic development of the country. Community development Projects, National Extension Services were launched. A chain of scientific laboratories, agricultural Research Institutions, Technical Institutions, a gigantic public sector of economy, were created. Means of transport and communication system such as railways, airways, waterways had been developed.

During the last few decades, India has made good economic progress in the field of Information Technology, Infrastructure, Agriculture, and other sectors. At present India is considered a major developing country with an average GDP growth rate of around 7 percent. In terms of nominal GDP, India is ranked seventh in the world.

During the last quarter of year 2014, India surprised the world by becoming the world's fastest growing major economy.

But in spite of all this progress, it cannot be said that the problem of national integration, social issues, poverty, income disparity, etc. has been solved. Industrialization is confined to few states and cities, and a bulk of rural areas are unaffected by industrialization. The society has been divided into two classes: A section of people who are below poverty line, and another section of people who have taken the advantages of all the developments.

The extremes of poverty are a hindrance in the process of national integration. Without a balanced economic growth and development, national unity cannot be achieved.

24
POVERTY IN INDIA

Poverty is defined as the condition in which individuals are deprived of basic amenities of life including food, clothing and shelter due to meagre amount of resources in hand. It is one of the major problems faced by the developing and underdeveloped nations all around the globe. It is widespread and has devastating effects on the growth and development of the economy. Poverty is one of the prominent reasons for the discussion amongst nations regarding communal wellbeing and harmony.

In a set up like India where majority of the population lives in the rural areas with scanty resources to survive, it becomes the responsibility of the government to bring about systematic changes in the standard of living of its citizens by introducing the requisite schemes and strategies and allocating the required expenditure to enhance the quality of their life. During 1950s, the official measures used by Indian government to measure the extent of poverty were based on food security and per capita income. But, with time the World Bank revised the standard parameters in order to study the multi-faceted aspect of poverty in an economy.

Two hundred years of the British rule stagnated the Indian economy to the core and flushed out most of its potential resources. Famines and mass deaths followed till India gained independence in the year 1947. But, the problem didn't end even then and poverty prevailed as an after-effect of it and still does.

It is said that rural India is the heart of India. In reality, the life of people living in rural areas is marked with severe poverty and in spite of all the efforts, the condition of poor villagers is worse. Rural elites migrate from rural to urban areas in search of employment and thus add to their burden. Majority of the population in rural India depends on agriculture to sustain their livelihoods .Thus, with the decline of agricultural productivity and industries; India needs an industrial and technological push by the government and international agencies in order to strive for the developmental goals. The significant reasons for increase in the level of poverty in India are explosion in population, dependence on agro-based income, high tax bars, unemployment, vicious cycle of middlemen, illiteracy, casteism and unequal distribution of wealth and natural resources. All these factors contribute to not only the extent of poverty in India but also lead to the marginalisation of communities and political instability in the economy.

The government has initiated various schemes in order to eradicate poverty, including subsidising food and other necessities, increased access to loans, improving agricultural techniques and price supports, and promoting family planning and education. Notable examples of poverty alleviation programmes include the Five year plans, The United Nations Millennium Development Goals (MDG), Mahatma Gandhi National Rural Employment Guarantee Act (MGNREGA), Midday Meal Scheme and Rural Housing Indira Awas Yojana (IHY). Also, international organisations like United Nations and World Bank insist on the development of human resource by investing the required expenditure on areas like education, healthcare, sanitation, food security and employment to improve the standard of living of the people; for the developed nations like India.

A lot of states like Bihar, Jharkhand and Madhya Pradesh in India have higher poverty rates. India projected a steady drop in the poverty rates from 51 percent in 1990 to 22 percent in 2015 by investing in the factors like employment opportunities, industrialisation, education, healthcare, etc. But, the gap between the rich and the poor and rural and urban India still prevails.

Therefore, poverty eradication must be the topmost priority of the government in order to come out from stagnation and achieve the set developmental goals. Eradication of poverty would guarantee a sustainable and inclusive growth of economy and society. Also, people will be encouraged to work more and develop themselves as individuals and as citizens of the nation to be able to be an asset to the economy and with that, crime rates might also fall.

25

RISING PRICES: PLIGHT OF A COMMON MAN

nflation is defined as constant increase in general price level of goods and services over a period of time in an economy. This phenomenon is widely experienced by people throughout the country since the year 1995. The era after independence has seen a variety of changes in the economic and societal status of the nation. Globalisation and westernisation are on its peak and new trends are emerging in the trade and industrial sector, new reforms are made and the liberalisation policies are being followed. The emerging trends and extension of trade for luxury goods see increase in demand for goods and services thereby, leading to what we call demand-pull inflation. The theory of rising prices can be understood from various other elements like supply of goods and services, etc.

We commonly experience rise in prices of necessary food items like onions, tomatoes, wheat flour, sugar, and other items like TV sets, mobile phones, medicines, etc. Industrialists and some people of the nation have a lot of resentment and anger regarding the problem. They hold the government responsible for the situation as 'Rising Prices' not only reduces the purchasing power of the people and discourages investment and savings but also it is a loss in real value in the medium of exchange and unit of account within the economy. But, on the other hand 'Rising Prices' helps in reducing the real burden of public and private debt by keeping nominal interest rates so that central banks can regulate interest rates to maintain stability in the economy, and reduce the rate of unemployment.

Increase in the taxes is yet another aspect that adds to the problem. Thus, the government must ensure a reasonable and systematic process of tax-levying from all the strata of the society. The problem of inflation has not spared anyone neither the rich nor the poor and the middle class families, the people with fixed income and wage earners are the worst affected by rising prices. The major reason for the rising prices is corruption, red tapism in the administration and population explosion that leads to increase in the aggregate demand of the people causing inflation.

Inflation is taking up the poverty line and poverty is not just economic but defined by way of health and education – Azim Premji

Inflation has a widespread impact on the working of the economy. It increases the gap between the rich and poor and people are not even able to purchase the basic necessities of life. Unemployment adds to the problem as the industries face the problem of fluctuations in the demand and supply of goods and services. Also, black marketing and hoarding act as cherry on the top. Manufacturers and wholesalers create excess demand of the commodities by artificial shortage of goods and services.

The government is constantly trying to minimise the problem by opening up Public Distribution System (Fair Price Shops) for some essential commodities needed for daily consumption which sells goods at subsidised and reasonable prices. Also, it is working on reducing unemployment, illiteracy, over population and corruption levels in the economy by implementing the required policies such as MGNREGA, RTE, etc.

26

UNEMPLOYMENT IN INDIA

Unemployment is defined as a situation in which capable people seeking for work do not get paid work. It is one of the major concerns and issue in the developing countries like India, China or Indonesia now a days.

India is home to 1.25 billion people and generating employment for each and every individual is a great concern. We have achieved advancement in almost every sector ranging from education (smart classes, etc.) to health (e-health, m-health) to agriculture (HYV seeds, fertilisers, pesticides, etc.) giving rise to the need of machineries more than manpower. The highly sophisticated machines are run by skilled and trained people and skilled workers are employed in these large industries. But the large masses of unskilled Indians find it hard to get a job that suits their skills. Thus, people working in agricultural and other related sectors that require high manpower have become unemployed. But on the other hand this situation has given rise to BPO and KPO based industries that provide employment to major part of the unemployed population. Individuals outsource their skills to the foreign world and get good returns. Multi National Corporations (MNCs) are yet another aspect related to globalisation to solve the problem of unemployment. MNCs set up their branches in developing countries like India in order to get manpower at lower costs and get quality work.

Economists have identified various patterns related to the problem of unemployment in India namely, voluntary

72

unemployment, involuntary unemployment, frictional unemployment, hidden unemployment, etc.

Voluntary unemployment refers to a situation wherein individuals get work but they are not willing to work at the given wages rate whereas involuntary unemployment refers to the situation wherein individuals are willing to work at the prevailing wage rate but they do not get work.

Frictional unemployment refers to the time spent between jobs when a worker is searching for, or transitioning from one job to another. Classical or real-wage unemployment is defined as a situation in which jobs are set above certain level, causing the number of job-seekers to exceed the number of vacancies. And cyclical unemployment occurs when there is not enough aggregate supply in the economy to provide jobs for everyone who wants to work.

Unemployment in India is an outcome of a lot of factors like population explosion, unwillingness to work at lower wage rates, gender wage inequality, illiteracy, and post industrialisation. It not only widens the gap between the rich and the poor but also erodes self-esteem by promoting social disturbances, unrest and conflict. It leads to economic instability in the economy as whole. Every individual contributes to the development and growth of the economy. Thus, development of an individual is directly proportional to the development of the economy.

Unemployment also increases vulnerability to cardiovascular disease, somatisation, anxiety, depression, and suicide. Moreover, unemployed people have higher rates of medication use, poor diet, physician visits, tobacco smoking, alcoholic beverage consumption, drug use, and lower rates of exercise.

Therefore, in order to curb the problem, the government of India must invest in health, education, etc. in order to make individuals fit to work, set up industries to enhance job opportunities and motivate the setting up of solo businesses by provision of loans at lower interest rates, lower taxes and subsidiaries especially in rural areas. Also, various programmes and schemes have come into existence like MGNREGA (Mahatama Gandhi National Rural Employment Guarantee Act), Deen Dayal Upadhaya Grameen Kaushalaya Yojna, Digital India programme, Gramin Bhandaran Yojna and Pradhan Mantri Kaushal Vikas Yojana, etc. which have helped curtail the problem.

27

GENERATION GAP AND ITS IMPACT ON SOCIETY

Generation gap refers to the difference in opinion, values and viewpoint amongst generations, especially between parents, grandparents and children. Every generation seems to be conflicting at one point or the other with its preceding and succeeding generation. Since parents and children are not born at the same time, the generation gap is an unavoidable occurrence.

The problem of generation gap is universal and everybody across the globe faces the unchangeable problem. But this problem is experienced intensely in countries like India or Gulf countries where the families live united. Although the families continue to live united, they may be in odd terms with each other. The unity that exists in a family system is a positive indication but it should not lead to negative consequences. The problem is experienced due to several reasons which should be properly analyzed.

In ancient world, parents were given the status of gods and their commands used to be the final words for their children to listen. But it is not so at present. The difference in generation gap that used to happen before and now is that at present, the generation gap is more. While children go wrong in treating their parents as people with old and outdated mindsets, parents also go wrong in ceasing to understand that their children too are independent individuals with their own thoughts. Children should not be forced or asked to follow the footsteps of their parents. They too have the right to take their own decisions sometimes.

There are several problems that lead to this conflicting problem. All the generations are brought up in an entire different way. As a result, their mental framework differs from each other. Physciological and behavorial patterns are formed on the basis of circumstances one undergoes. When the people of the different generations meet each other, they often are induced to difference in opinion, communication gap, conflicts etc.

Due to the difference in mental framework the likes and dislikes also differ from each other. In this way both the parties cannot live in peace with each other and they are unable to respect the likes and opinion of each other.

The frequency of thoughts flow from opposite directions in a parallel manner. When the thought process from the two parties is so different, then love cannot be expressed even if it exists between the two parties. Both of them are unable to find a proper channel to express their feelings also. In this way gap creates between the two relationships.

Generation gap occurs between parents and children or between in-laws. It also occurs between teachers and students but the degree of gap is less because they do not spend much time with each other. This problem leads to communication gap and the two parties are unable to understand the channel for communication.

Due to emotional incompatibility, arguments over silly matters and conflicts began to occur often frequently. The peace in the premises of the house is disturbed.

In the extreme cases, the parties even decide to abandon each other. The children decide to leave the house of the parents due to lack of emotional space constantly. The daughter-in-law may provoke her husband to abandon her mother-in-law for disability to cope up unreasonable demands.

Realization and a high level of understanding is one of the optimal solutions to combat the problem. Both the parties should often discuss openly about their childhood and the funny and sad incidents that took place during their childhood days. The two parties can understand the lifestyle of each other. Both the generations should not think high about themselves. They should understand their own limitations and that they both depend upon each other at some point or the other.

They both should realize that the peace can be established through co-operation. Everybody should develop the attribute of respecting each other. To build a close relationship with each other, the two generations should enjoy periodically by going out for a cinema, restaurants, shopping and many other fun-filled activities. Both the parties should purposely spend time with each other whenever they are free. This activity creates an emotional bondage very quickly.

28

HAS INDIA LOST ITS CULTURAL ROOTS

Indian Culture, which is one of the oldest and richest cultures, is nowadays posing a serious threat because western culture is influencing the youths in India and is slowly and gradually wiping the Indian culture. The western culture can be seen in Metros and it is slowly heading towards urban, semi-urban, and even rural India.

The culture of India is based not only on its long history, unique geography and diverse demography, but on its ancient heritages also. Some historians believe that our culture is the oldest culture on the Earth. The Indian tradition dates back to 8,000 BC and has a continuous recorded history for over 2,500 years.

Due to globalization and commercialization, the rich culture of India is disappearing day by day. Our culture has a spiritual base whereas the Western culture is based on materialistic factors and has impacted the youths the most.

The westernization of India has greatly affected traditions, customs, and family values. Today, the respect for elders and others has greatly decreased due to decreasing moral values of people. The joint families are broken because they want to live separate from each other. In traditional Indian culture, one has to care and support other family members. Also in today's situation both husband and wife are working, so there is no one at home to look after the children. Many times a child is being taken care of by someone else. Children are not getting rich cultural values which their parents have had. Slowly, all customary Indian values are diminishing and everyone is moving onto a more western culture.

Now-a-days nobody bothers about others and only cares about oneself which is totally contradictory to our Indian culture which teaches to be a part of each other's joys and sorrows to celebrate the moments together and share the grief together.

People prefer to speak in English rather than in their native language. They prefer to wear western outfits over Indian traditional ones. They listen to western music and forget Indian classical form of music. Even in Indian classical, dance has taken a back stage and hip-hop, contemporary and swag are practiced largely by people. The lack of morals, the lacking faith in God, late night parties, the influence of drugs and alcohols, least interest in Indian languages like Sanskrit, Hindi, celebrating mother's day, father's day, valentine day, fools' day etc. rather than celebrating our Indian festivals and focusing on being independent at an early age. These are all a big Influence of western culture.

However, despite westernization in India, people still follow their culture and are attached to their roots. Even today Indian families treat the guests as gods and serve them even in tough times. In our tradition, a guest should never leave the house hungry. The respect towards the elderly is still there and is a major factor in the culture. The elderly pass on their stories and their experiences to their grandchildren. Even though we have a fancy for fast food, we still love our traditional dishes. On special occasions we Indian prefer to wear traditional clothes over western clothes and follow traditional customs. We still love to celebrate Holi and Diwali with enthusiasm.

The modernization of India is a good thing but the cultural values of India need to be maintained. Even though the Indian people have improved their way of life, their principles and beliefs have remained constant and their feelings have been attached with our cultural values. A person can alter his clothing or foods he eats, but his deep understanding and commitment to the culture will never be taken away.

29
IMPACT OF MEDIA ON THE YOUTH

Media in the form of newspaper, magazines, radio, television, internet etc. is playing a significant role in spreading awareness on general to specific issues, and in providing information on sensational matters of national and international importance and current affairs among common mass. It brings forth a platform for the people, which they can relate to, where they cannot only read but also hear and feel at the same time. It has a widespread impact on them. Media provides for it users a platform of expression.

In a country like India where majority of the population is illiterate, TV not only entertains but also informs and educates the people. It helps in building a strong foundation for the citizens of the nation by making individuals aware about the current events happening in the country and around the world.

India is a secularly democratic nation. Thus, communication has always been the utmost crucial area of concern.

There has been tremendous advancement in the media industry starting from the telegraph, to the radio, to the newspapers to magazines and now to the internet. The teenagers or youngsters are the most affected by it both positively and negatively. On one hand, where it provides them with all the information that they require and equip them with social and practical skills on the other, it also makes them brand conscious and open to a lot of obnoxious and inappropriate stuff . Sexual content in advertisements, magazines, radio programmes and television shows are a few examples of obscene stuff.

Current researches have helped discover that people suffering from social seclusion can employ various media like television, radio, etc. in order to create what is known a para-social or faux relationship with characters from their favourite shows and movies as a way of overcoming their feelings of isolation and social deprivation.

Media serves as a channel of cultural expression which informs, educates and entertains individuals. It links the whole world together in the form of globalization.

Advertising is an essential aspect of media industry. It plays major role in generating the revenue with due advertising. One can glimpse thousands of advertisements on various mass media platforms today. Ads on TV, magazines and newspapers appear very interesting and catchy to the individuals due to their visual appeal. These ads not only convey about the product and services but also serve as a measure to educate and inform people about the problems of the masses as a whole. But, a lot of them contain inappropriate content and images of women in unfitting postures and facade in them which in turn affects the mindset of the youngsters and hinder their growth prospects. It even leads them to committing a lot of crimes like rape, robbery, etc.

Media acts as a catalyst of change and a gatekeeper of the society. It helps create awareness about issues that are crucial to the wellbeing of mankind. It not only affects the opinions but also persuades the citizens to think accordingly.

Mass Media is a mighty informative weapon of modern epoch. Every day people all over the world watch TV, read newspapers, listen to the radio and, use Internet and this way perceive information, widespread by the mass media. Young people are greatly influenced by the mass media. Alcohol advertisements, cigarettes and junk food have negative impact on young adults and children. In addition, violence transmitted through different types of mass media created additional problem. All the problems mentioned above underline the importance of study the impact of mass media on the youth. Different scholars underline the necessity of different facts, which reflect the scope of the problem. "Additional effort is needed to develop theories that can identify underlying processes and mechanisms that link media influences to outcomes. Outcomes in turn call for tools that can measure, evaluate, and help explain how certain media experiences influence, and are influenced by, health and behavioral factors as well as cognitive and developmental processes" (Beatty). Negative impacts of the mass media on children are out of doubt.

30

IMPORTANCE OF MORAL VALUES

Good moral values are the basis of strong character and dominant personality. These values make us a good human being who is able to understand the sufferings of those in need. Moral values allow us to have an overall feeling of peace and joy. These values give real meaning and purpose to the life of a person. We can build a strong character by maintaining good societal values.

Every individual understands that life is important; hence he or she needs moral values, which act as guiding principles. Children are taught to show respect to elders and other people. Moral values are a reflection of an individual character and spirituality. Parents strive to instil these values in children because they tend to learn by observing what other people do.

Moral values help in improving behaviour, instilling respect and enhancing relationships with others. Knowing what is right or wrong is an important element in life that shapes the character of an individual. Good moral values allow a person to make the right decisions and improve their interactions with other people.

Incorporating the moral value of honesty in one's life makes one trustworthy. One will have a clear conscience because he can respect himself. In addition to honesty, one also needs to incorporate moral value of compassion into one's life. Compassion allows us to have sympathy for other people. When someone is compassionate, people are more likely to put their trust in you because they will be non-judgmental of their circumstances. Thirdly, the moral value of courage gives you the determination to face anything that impedes your progress through life.

In life it is essential to be modest as modesty allows us to realize what our limits are. It helps us to stay focused and keeps us away from becoming overconfident and reckless. People will feel comfortable because one is humble and he doesn't try to belittle them. It is also important to incorporate moral value of forgiveness. Forgiveness gives us peace and help to recover from the past hurtful or damaging situations. It allows us to abandon feelings of anger or resentment against others or yourself.

Respecting the elders, neighbours, and the sick and other people within society helps to enhance re-lationships. As people get older, they need care and assistance where possible. Good relationships help to create a good coexistence between people. At work-places, people need to learn how to relate with both juniors and seniors. Being honest helps a person to be recognized and achieve his or her goals in work easily.

Moral values have an important role in the stability of marriages and families. Partners should be truthful to one another and solve problems wisely to avoid a divorce. Standing firm on what is right no matter the situation is always a courageous decision that improves the quality of life.

In conclusion, moral values are extremely important for your overall development of personality and well-being of a person. Moral values provide a structure for your life. Honesty makes you good and respectable in the society.

31

NUCLEAR FAMILY vs JOINT FAMILY

In India, the joint family system has been in existence since ancient times. The father is considered as the head of the family. The parents, sons, daughters-in-law and grandchildren together constitute a joint family. The head of the family feels proud of the large family. However, with the passage of time the joint family system has disintegrated giving rise to the nuclear family system.

The nuclear family consists of a man, his wife and their children. The job opportunities available in the cities become the main cause of disintegration of the joint family system. People migrate to the cities in search of jobs. For a number of reasons, a joint family system cannot exist in the cities. There is a lack of living space in the cities. It is difficult to accommodate all members of a joint family in a single house. The cost of living is very high in the cities. It is generally believed that mother-in-law and daughter-in-law do not get along well in a city household.

In ancient and medieval times, the older members of the family enjoyed great respect. They stayed and relaxed with each other and also amused themselves with the pranks of their grandchildren. They handled financial matters of the household. But with the rise of towns and cities, the older and younger generations widened a great deal. A survey carried out in Delhi revealed that 40 % of the elderly people have no caretakers. They spend their old age away from the love and care of their children and grandchildren. There has been a steep rise in the crime rate against senior citizens. Old age homes have been set up at various places to take care of senior citizens. In Delhi, Police are making a list of helpless senior citizens to make arrangements for their safety.

The nuclear family gives a lot of freedom from traditions, orthodoxy and old ways of life. Hence, whenever the parents and grown-up children cannot get along well, and if adult children can afford, they prefer to build a separate house and form a nuclear family. There is also an urge to build a house which one may call one's own. As this happens, with most of the changes in society, initially the people from the old system do not take this change very well. They are saddened to see disintegration of the family and erosion of old values.

A nuclear family also has many advantages. In a nuclear family, the mother is able to look after the needs of her children well. She can take care of their personal needs in a much better way than she could do in a joint family. The family earns, spends and saves money for itself. Parents can invest money for the education of their children. They can put them in good schools and provide them with better career opportunities. They can understand one another well. But in the joint family system, children don't get individual attention. The womenfolk never find time to look after their children for they remain busy in the household work. Children are not educated much as they join the family occupation. The womenfolk face many restrictions, disharmony occurs because of the size of the family.

Today the youth crave for name, fame and wealth. In the nuclear family with working parents, sometimes the youth receives no guidance from their parents. They turn to friends for advice. Many a time, friends misguide them. They are misled. In the joint family system, the older members are likely to guide the young ones. Being old and experienced, they are able to provide solutions to their problems. The older generation should be revered. They are an asset to the society.

The media is somewhat responsible for disintegration of the joint-family system. It often portrays the mother-in-law as a threat to the well-being of the young bride. In some movies, she is shown to influence her son against the young bride. Many of the serials broad-casted on television portray negative aspect of elders. Newspapers also report about gruesome acts committed in some families. The foreign media has instilled western and liberal views in the youth. All these factors curb the development of the family as a close knit unit. The media should try to restore the lost image of the old family system.

The advantage of the joint family system outweighs the disadvantages. In the cycle of life, one certainly reaches old age and faces the same problems as his parents or grandparents have undergone. So, old parents and grandparents should not be deprived of the love and care of the near and dear ones.

Moreover, different strengths of different family members can uplift the family and it can provide a sense of fulfilment to the family as a whole. The joint family can become a training ground for the future generations to learn and develop attribute and skills of living in harmony with other citizens in the society. If our family model is based on tolerance, togetherness and warmth, it will be reflected positively in the society at large.

32

PEN IS MIGHTIER THAN SWORD

The power of a pen is tremendously mightier than that of a sword. What a sharp-edged sword can't achieve can be achieved by the help of a minute tip of a pen. It implies that the power of writing is much stronger than the power of hatred, war and fighting. A war always ends in killing and has only tragic ending - defeat, death, loss. There is no end of the tunnel when a war is there, and even if it comes, there is no light.

Early man lived on the basis of the strength of his muscle power. In the struggle for existence, it was the survival of the fittest. Gradually, man became civilized and progressed in various fields. The destinies of nations were shaped by wars. Later on man realized that the use of weapons could not solve problems. Weapons could kill a man but could not bring about a change of heart.

Ideas have a much larger impact than violence. Force is incapable of changing the ideas and beliefs of the people. When people are influenced by new ideas, changes occur in the society. Ideas are propagated by writing. Brave deeds and valour shown in the battlefield are certainly praiseworthy. But no clash of arms could achieve what great men through their writing have archived.

The invention of the written word has helped man to store and propagate his thoughts, beliefs, and ideas. After the development of the printing press by Johanns Guttenberg , the printed word became the most powerful medium of propagating the same. Newspapers became a mighty weapon. Public opinion is generally built up not by clash of arms but by the writings of great men and by newspapers. The pen has been able to make the people stand up against tyranny and injustice.

Ideas are expressed through the power of the pen. The written word makes a permanent impact on several generations. It moulds life according to the times. Violence can only suppress the beliefs of the people. The pen stands for positive and constructive efforts, while the sword signifies negative postures and destruction all around. The sword can force them into submission but cannot propagate an idea. Pen can solve many complex issues. The sword can only destroy. Wars have no significant impact on the development of a nation.

We have inherited spiritual books like the Gita, the Bible, the Quran, the beautiful poetry by great poets like Wordsworth, T.S. Eliot, Keats and others and the wisdom of Carlye, Marx, Kautilya and Chanakya because of pen. These achievements have guided and brought solace to innumerable people all over the world.

The pen is mainly an instrument of peace but the sword is an instrument of war. It is a weapon of violence whether it is used for offence or defense. It is the cause of innumerable deaths of innocent men, women and children in war. This is evident from the causalities suffered in the two World Wars and in our own time, the Iran-Iraq War, which was fought for so many years.

33

RIGHT TO EDUCATION

The whole purpose of education is to turn mirrors into windows – Sydney J. Harris

Education is the key aspect of a developed economy. It not only makes people aware about their rights but also helps in putting their potentials to optimum use by opening up opportunity windows of the outside world before them. Education plays a vital role in the upbringing of individuals and society as a whole. And in a country like India, where majority of the population is illiterate, it is utmost important for the citizens and government to realise its worth and spread awareness about the issue.

India is one of the 135 countries where right to education is one the fundamental rights provided to each and every citizen who fall under the specified age category. But, as per the supreme court of India, minority institutions are exempted from it. During the speech, the then prime minister of India, Manmohan Singh outlined the significance of education in the developmental process by saying, "We are committed to ensuring that all children, irrespective of gender and social category, have access to education. An education that enables them to acquire skills, knowledge, values and attitudes necessary to become responsible and active citizens of India."

The Right of Children to Free and Compulsory Education Act was enacted on 4th August, 2009 by the parliament of India under Article 21A of the Indian constitution. It focuses on the need and importance of free and compulsory education for children between six to fourteen years of age in India.

The act prohibits the following practices:

(i)   physical punishment and mental harassment

(ii) screening procedures for admission of children

(iii) capitation fee

(iv) private tuition by teachers

(v) running of schools without recognition

Under the act, all private schools are required (except the minority institutions) to reserve 25% of seats for the poor and other categories of children (to be reimbursed by the state as part of the public-private partnership plan). The Act also offers that no child shall be held back, expelled, or required to pass a board examination until the completion of elementary education. There is also a provision for special training of school drop-outs to bring them up to par with students of the same age. The right to education for children with disabilities until 18 years of age is given under a separate legislation- the Persons with Disabilities Act.

The Ministry of HRD and the ministry of 14-member of National Advisory Council including Kiran Karnik, former president of NASSCOM, Krishna Kumar, former director of the NCERT, Mrinal Miri, former vice-chancellor of North-East Hill University, Yogendra Yadav – social scientist India, Sajit Krishnan Kutty Secretary of The Educators Assisting Children's Hopes (TEACH) India, Annie Namala, an activist and head of Centre for Social Equity and Inclusion and Aboobacker Ahmad, vice-president of Muslim Education Society, Kerala implemented the act.

On the first anniversary of the act, surveys were conducted to present the real status of country's educational system which still lacks 508,000 teachers and admits that still 8.1 million children remain out of school nationwide.

The Right to Education Act aims to provide quality and free education to all children as their fundamental right. It envisages them to build a better and stable career for them to live in. Therefore, it is now our responsibility to make correct use of the liberties provided to us and ensure the implementation of the Act in true spirits so that the children between six to fourteen years of age can get education free of cost irrespective of their caste, creed, religion and language.

34

SOCIAL NETWORKING :
PROS AND CONS

No matter if you are searching for a former college roommate, your first grade teacher, or an international friend, no easier or faster way to make a connection exists than social media. Although Facebook, Twitter, LinkedIn and Pinterest are probably the most well-known social networking communities, new websites are popping up regularly that let people connect and interact over the Web. With each of these sites, individuals can make new friends, build business connections or simply extend their personal base by connecting and interacting with friends of friends - which can have a multiplying effect.

When you opt to participate in a social network community, you can pick and choose individuals whose likes and dislikes are similar to yours and build your network around those commonalities. For instance, if you are a chess enthusiast, a book lover or have a particular political leaning, you can find and interact with those who share your interest.

Many social networking sites incorporate an instant messaging feature, which lets people exchange information in real-time via a chat. This is a great feature for teachers to use and facilitate classroom discussions because this feature lets them utilize the vast store of information available on the Web. It saves a lot of time for the teacher since students no longer need to visit a library to conduct research and it can be a great way to engage distracted learners.

School is not the only setting where this type of re-al-time information sharing can be beneficial. Social networking can provide a tool for managers to utilize in team meetings, for conference organizers to update attendees and for business people to use as a means of interacting with clients or prospects. Some leaders make use of Tweets or other social media updates during presentations. This approach can make events more interactive and help the presenter reach a larger audience.

Undoubtedly, social networking has revolutionized the speed of news cycle. Most news channels now rely on social media sites to collect and share information. Social media, especially Twitter, is steadily becoming a mainstream source for breaking news. Today, an individual can know, in no time, what is happening throughout the world. This has led to the development of a nearly instantaneous news cycle as everything from terrorist attacks to local car crashes get shared on social media, quickly alerting their intended audience of the event.

But, as a coin has two sides social networking sites have disadvantages as well. When potentially offensive content is posted online, the amount of feedback can be excessive and is often brutal. This is particularly true with highly opinionated subjects like politics and religion.

Use of social networks may expose individuals to other forms of harassment or even inappropriate contact. This can be especially true for teens and younger children. Unless parents diligently filter the Web content their family views, children could be exposed to pornography or other inappropriate content.

Also, whether you like it or not, the information you post on the Internet is available to almost anyone who is clever enough to access it. Most thieves need just a few vital pieces of personal information to make your life a nightmare.

Thus, when using any social media platform, take responsibility for your own safety and never join a group just because it is trendy or all your friends are doing it. In evaluating the advantages and disadvantages of social networking, it's essential to be cautious and protect your privacy. Be careful with what you post and treat others as if you were in a face-to-face situation.

35

THE EVIL OF DOWRY

"Any young man, who makes dowry a condition to marriage, discredits his education and his country and dishonours womanhood". – Mahatama Gandhi

India is the land of customs and religions with marriage being one of the most auspicious occasions in the life of an individual. Marriage is celebrated with utmost zeal and joyfulness. All the relatives and acquaintances get together for the ceremonial event. This occasion establishes a bond and reflects on the forthcoming life of bride and groom and all the people gathered at the event bless them with open hearts. It is not only the groom and bride but also their families who share beautiful bond and get tied for lifetime.

But, what if this auspicious event is blemished by some old age custom of dowry. In the giving past, parental properties and gifts were given to the brides from their maternal side on their marriage, which steadily and unfortunately took the shape of dowry and ruined women's lives. Dowry significantly refers to the practice of parental property in the name of gifts at the marriage of a daughter. The practice can be seen in almost all the countries today. Dowries are demanded by many families now a days in areas like Asia, Northern Africa and the Balkans. The Africans characterise these gifts as "bride price". And if they are not given, it usually takes the form of violence against women, including killings and acid attacks.

The custom of dowry predates to the Babylon where it is intended to offer lifetime security to the bride as per the family affordability and it was governed by the husband as part of the family assets. But, in India the practice was not noticed until the Vedic period. Women in ancient India had property inheritance rights only by appointment or when they had no brothers.

Dowry may include cash, jewellery, electrical appliances, furniture, bedding, crockery, utensils, car and other household items that help the newly-weds set up their home. Even though it is illegal by law it is still practiced in almost all religions from Hindus to Muslims (Jahez). In India, it is illegal to demand for or give dowry under the Dowry Prohibition Act, 1961 in Indian civil law and subsequently by Sections 304B and 498a of the Indian Penal Code (IPC).

Kirti Singh, a famous scholar states, "Dowry is widely considered to be both a cause and a consequence of son preference. The practice of dowry inevitably leads to discrimination in different areas against daughters and makes them vulnerable to various forms of violence including dowry-related violence, marital rape, female genital mutilation and other traditional practices harmful to women."

Dowry is a bane to the society. It exploits a woman and her family to the full but, even then people indebt themselves and do whatever it takes to fulfil the wishes of the groom and his family in the hope that it would help better the fortune of their daughter, which unfortunately turns out to be even worse by the increasing demands for dowry. Sometimes, even if the groom doesn't aim at demanding dowry the families force him to the act. Therefore, in order to stop the heinous crime, the boys and girls must take pledge to stop the wrong practice in India and the world as a whole.

36

VOCATIONAL STUDIES

Vocational education, or career and technical education, is an elective program that provides middle, high school, and adult learners with training in a particular career. Vocational education can take place at the secondary, post-secondary, further education, and at higher education level; and can interact with the apprenticeship system. At the post-secondary level, vocational education is often provided by highly specialized trade and technical schools.

Every man must have a vocation – a trade, a business, or a profession – in order to earn his livelihood. There are institutions for imparting various types of specialized training to help men qualify for this. The specialist is in demand everywhere, in the office as well as in factories, and even in educational institutions.

There are schools for teaching medicine and engineering, accountancy and computer science. There are as many types of institutions for imparting vocational training as there are vocations. A person trained in one of these institutions will find greater scope to show his merits than one untrained. This is more than ever so today when vocations are multiplying, but ceased to be hereditary and child labour is becoming unlawful.

An untrained man in the modern world may even be a liability or burden to the society. He is a quack; he knows only the 'how' of things; he has no idea of its 'why'. Hence, if there is any trouble anywhere, breakdown in a machine, or mistake in a ledger, a mat-functioning of the gadget, he only pleads helplessness, grumbles and patches up the trouble anyhow, leading to a more serious fault. In reality there is no place for the untrained worker, in these days of specialised work.

The successful careers require varying levels of education, with some students gaining enough training to enter the workforce immediately following high school, while others may require a four-year college degree. Students may elect to take only a single course or a concentration in a particular trade. The areas of concentration most frequently offered by vocational education programs focus on business, trade and industry, health, agriculture, family and consumer sciences, marketing, and technology.

In all technically advanced countries, like England, America, Russia, Germany, Japan – only a few are encouraged to go up for a general education. The majority of youngsters have to attend a preparatory school till their eighteenth year or thereabout, and then join some vocational school. It may be a technical school for learning the intricacies of bookkeeping and accountancy or handling a computer. Hence there is now craze for a specialised degree. It must be some school that makes him a specialist; otherwise, he finds himself handicapped in the struggle for earning a decent living.

In our country, vocational education is yet to become popular. Very few students go in for the vocational stream in the High School course; also very insignificant arrangements are made for it. They are expensive too. In most cases too much stress is laid on theory. In a good system, theory and practice must be combined. To ensure this, along with class-work, there must be proper arrangements for ensuring practical training in a factory or a firm. The apprenticeship system, which attaches a boy to a firm or a factory, has some admirable features. In Russia, technical classes are attached to factories and agricultural farms, which provide workers with excellent opportunities for improving their knowledge and skill.

37

AN INDIAN TEMPLE

In India, there are many beautiful temples. People in large numbers go to temples everyday. Different religions, cultures have different kinds of temples and ways of performing their rituals. Temples of South India are known for their magnificence and huge size. The Cola, Panda and Cheri kings considered building temples as their mission of life. Building these temples involved their feelings of devoutness towards their god and goddesses so much that they kept on building them.

Earlier, temples were not only for worshipping but they were centres for assembling of the people for discussions on social developments. Temples follow the principles of good conduct and discipline. The main reason for increase in violence among people these days is because they are neglecting the spiritual aspect of life. Temples form an essential part in the development of our moral thoughts which are responsible for making people honest, open-minded, liberal and full of feelings.

Thoughts of temples and God add discipline and peace in our lives and make us realize the value of our life. Meditating sitting in a temple increases our concentration level and connects us with our soul. In South India, there are very huge and beautiful temples. The main temple of Lord Vishnu at Mridangam is perhaps the biggest temple in Tamil Nadu. Many priests and devotees sing devotional songs on Sri Ranganatha of Mridangam. Tirupati is a small temple town built by a king, and devotees throng the temple regularly.

101

Once when I visited Tirupati, I had to stand in a long queue with hundreds of people waiting to enter the temple and to worship Lord Venkateswara. Devotees give money as a charity for the temple and its care- takers. You can always find a large number of people, tourists, and students, who come to worship Lord Vishnu, the Lord of the seven hills, in days and nights.

The Tirupati range is a very long range of hills. Several kinds of ritualistic worship of Lord Vishnu go on throughout the day. Only expert drivers can drive the buses or cars through the way of temples. Many other mountains and hills have roads leading to the top. Buses and cars can go up the roads which have *harapan* bends.

Everyday is a day of worshiping in Tirupati. When devotees come out of the sanctum sanctorum after worship, sweets, curd rice, tamarind rice, coconut rice, doughnut or some other eatables are given. Eatables offered to the Lord, especially Ladd and doughnuts, are available at the vendors stall.

There are hundreds of small cottages where people can stay. The temple town has a large floating population and people who visit Tirupati get a feel of joy. It is so much fun to go to Tirupati and worship Lord Vishnu and others gods too. It gives a totally unique experience. It can be compared to the Vatican City which is a city hallowed by the memories of Christ and where the Pope has his palace. One must visit to these beautiful temples built all over India once to get a lifetime experience, to know about the glory of the God concerned, and to comprehend the contemporary society through a keen eye.

38

A VISIT TO A HISTORICAL BUILDING - SAFDARJUNG'S TOMB

"You employ stone, wood and concrete, and with these materials you build houses and places, that is construction. But when you suddenly touch my heart, you do me good and make me say "This is beautiful, that is architecture."

Some days leave an everlasting impact on your heart and soul. Life gets a fresh breathe when history rises from its grave. It happened with me on April 9th, while my school friends and I visited Safdarjung's Tomb. The tomb was built for Safdarjung, the prime minister of Mughal Emperor Muhammad Shah. It was built in 1754 in the Mughal style and is described as the "last flicker in the lamp of Mughal architecture". We all were mesmerized by the beauty of architectural masterpiece. Any time you spend with your friends is sure to be a fun and a visit to such a beautiful place for sure adds one more memory to your experience.

The tomb still gives a mystique feeling. The central tomb has a huge tomb. There are four water canals leading to the four corners of the building: one has an ornately decorated gateway while the other three corners have octagonal towers. The canals are four oblong tanks, one on each side of the tomb. On the whole, the tomb has been decorated with cheap material, pointing to the economic conditions of that time.

Some people may say that it is not that big or lacks something special in it but it is right in front of your eyes and you are not able to notice it. The fusion of different architectural style in a way makes this monument very special. Every aspect of the monument reflects other earlier monuments. For example, the entrance reminds us of the Rajputana style whereas the main dome is taken from Taj Mahal.

But negligence and ignorance of anything can change it into worst, even the paradise into hell. Today, it is in a dilapidated condition, with cracks in the walls and the tomb's walls turning yellowish grey from white. The tomb has lost its pristine beauty. A monument which was so beautifully built with so much of hard work and also which reminds us of our culture is in tatters and what is left is only the glimpse of the glory. The worst part you will find in the whole area is its most important part where the grave lies. It looks so dirty as if it was cleaned years ago. It feels so sad from inside seeing our monuments in dilapidated condition. The immediate action and care is required to protect our national heritage. But in spite of this, I realized that the people in those times were full of life and were fond of unique architectural beauty.

39

MY BEST FRIEND

Friendship is the most amazing and beautiful bond of one's life with another. A true friendship is a god's gift. The one who has a best friend in her life is the luckiest of all. You feel empty in the absence of a true companion. Man is a social animal and s/he demands love and care. Therefore, s/he needs a true friend, which is forever. And I too can have this feeling, because I have world's best friend.

I still remember the first meeting with my best friend, at the backside of our college. I got to know him through a friend. We shook hands and moved on. As the time passed, and the chats increased, I found in him a person who is so lovable and honest. And slowly and gradually, we became best friends!

Best friends are our secret diaries. They know about every single secret which sometimes becomes too dangerous when one starts blackmailing the other. Oh God! They know about our likes and dislikes. They are so good listeners as they listen to our every single thing, whether good or bad.

Whether a good day or bad, this friendship has always got us closer and made the bond strong. My best friend, whom I call Mani, is not just a 'best friend' by name. He is one! He is gem of a person. Like any family member, he knows what sort of a person I am. He knows me so well, from both outside and inside. He is someone who can easily feel the moods in which I am. In every situation, he is always there to support me.

He is a very entertaining, helpful and honest person

at heart, but a guy who has changed the definition of a man. Strange! Yes, I reacted the same when I got to know him very well. He likes to go shopping, he loves beauty products as he loves himself so much. In our relation, he behaves like a girl and I like a man. I wish I could use emotions here to express my feelings. But anyhow, he is the cutest of all. He is a guy, having the 'understanding of others' quality in him, especially me, which makes me say ' I am proud of him' because nobody won't be able to find a guy like him in today's world.

He made my college life so much fun! From going to the college and returning back, I was always scared of what he will do as he is naughty number one. Though I enjoyed his company to the fullest, the sad part is, he graduated and left me alone to get boring. Yes! He is my senior.

He respects my feelings and helps me always. Many things of us like hobbies, likes and dislikes, etc are similar. We love listening to music, watching cartoons and playing carom at home. We take care of each other in the school and playground. We share notebooks and help each other whenever one of us remain absent in the class. We love drawing sceneries and arts in our spare time. We go at tour and picnic with our parents together in every winter and summer vacation.

But no worries! He is always there whenever I need him. And as he loves spending time talking with my mother, he comes anytime at home to surprise me. He is a friend, who is very similar to me. He is a person, who is down to earth. He finds happiness in small things like I do. He is the definition of a true best friend!

A best friend is someone with whom you've shared your secrets and laughed the loudest. A true friend probably knows you better than anyone else, like your parents, better than yourself too. Best friends are truly responsible for making your life worth living. Not only are they always up for the fun times but they are also the ones who are there for us when we need them the most.

40

MY FAMILY

Family is the place where you learn your first lesson of life. Your family members are the only assets that will stay with you forever. I am attached to my family very much and everyone in my family is well educated and has a lovely nature.

I live in a nuclear family of five members. My father is a property dealer. He always talks about some or the other properties and its rates. He is the leader of our family, and my superhero. He performs his duties with honesty. He is generous and liberal. He is almost busy. On holidays, he takes us for vacations or to shopping malls. He also takes interest in our education. I love my father.

My mother is an all rounder. She is a housewife as well as owns a workshop in which she does her stitching work for big showrooms boutique. She is a pretty lady, who plans the family budget and takes care of the whole family. She is not very modern by her dressing sense but by her mindset. She is a religious woman. She goes to the temple every morning. On sacred days, she takes all of us to the temple. She is the finest lady.

My grandmother is the sweetest person of all. Because of her, everybody has to get up early in the morning. She is fond of making sweet dishes and we love what she cooks. She is a disciplined lady and because of her everything needs to be in order.

My brother, who is younger to me, is the naughtiest of all. He studies in Xth standard and is fond of cooking. He loves to play football and is a gadget freak. He doesn't like to study much but is a very sweet and gentleman.

Although I am a student of final year, my family treats me like a child. No one calls me by my original name. I am ' raaje' for them. But this gives me a feel of so much love and care. I want to become the support system of my family. They have done a lot for me. Now it's time to repay all the love and care.

My family is the best family. Whatever the situations are, we are always there for each other to encourage. Good values and good morals are taught in our family. As kids, we are taught to respect our elders and love the ones who are younger to us.

I learn a lesson everyday from my grandmother, about honesty, punctuality, kindness etc. I love my family because they are gems of my life. They work hard so that we can get whatever we want makes me love and respect my parents even more. We play games every night, talk on various topics to spend some quality time together. Even my friends love my family. They love to spend time at my home with my parents, grandmother and brother. I love my family more than anyone else.

41

RESPECT FOR ELDERS

"Respect your Elders, Learn from the People who have Walked the Path before you respect them because Someday and Sooner than you could ever Imagine you are going to be Old too."

Respect your elders! We all are taught this in our childhood. But is it being really followed these days? Every day we see in newspapers or on television the kind of discrimination against the old and wise.

Different people have different beliefs and opinions on this issue. Respect for elders and grandparents have been a judgmental subject from ancient time. Some believe that respect should be earned and cannot be given freely. Contradictions among the people are born from individual's nature and behavior.

Respect is a feeling of deep admiration for some-one or something elicited by their abilities, qualities, or achievements. It is also behaving well with our elders with good gesture, moral, and gratitude. Respect is counted upon factors like honesty, truthfulness, goodness, gener-osity, behavior, moral, character, integrity etc. of a human being. If someone exhibits these values in them fully or partly, then s/he is a respectable person.

India has an ancient culture in which respect for elders holds a prime position. There are still joint families in India who are headed by its elders. We blindly respect them as they brought us in existence and because they are our elders in family tree. And you can see the kind of love and unity these families have. Parents who have taught their children to respect their grandparents will for sure earn respect of their grandchildren too.

We expect these values in everybody. Not only in house but everywhere. We can even give respect to a road side stranger but when it comes to our parents and grandparents, we generally don't apply these values and morals. People behave in such a way as if they are a burden on them but will they form a good image in the society? Therefore, it is clear that there is a role of selfishness. If a person other than our family is asked to examine our family members in public sense, then he might find out some or many inhuman values.

An Ideal human being is a person who comes above these judgmental thoughts and opinions and showcases goodness of elders in public to prove his values and culture at best. Therefore, every elders and grandparents should be respected because they are seniors in our society and they have lived through things that we can hardly imagine in our lives. They are more experienced than us and know the negatives and positives of everything.

But it does not mean that respecting an elder who gives inhuman values is also in our culture. Never respect a drinker, addict, thief or any bad elements of a person in a society or even if they belong to your family because it reduces the values, cultures and integrity of our society.

One thing is clear that respecting our elders increases our good '' karma'' and results in our better and successful future. It also creates your brand as a gentleman in the society. These types of people have higher success rate in our society. Therefore it can be concluded that respecting grandparents, elders and even younger is very fruitful, living and to establish cordial relations.

42

TELEVISION IN OUR DAILY LIFE

Today, television is very essential and important part of our life In fact, television has become so essential that one cannot imagine his or her life without TV. The sitcoms, soap operas which are shown on TV are loved by the viewers. To understand how important television is, we can look at different categories of programs and valuable content it offers and different purposes it serves in daily life. TV provides a lot of useful information and entertains through various types of programs.

First of all, there are a variety of programs which are broadcasted on television. Viewers can see a weather report and get prepared for the day. Information about the current situation of the country, what's going on can be seen on various news channels. Cartoons are the most entertaining programs for children where a child can enjoy programs and learn many different things. Cartoon Network, Pogo, Hungama are the names of few cartoon channels. Sports provide relaxation and fun to the young people and elders too, who are sports freak. School programs, news channels and different categories of teaching programs tell us about the world and help us to learn something new.

Television also shows advertisements. Ads tell us about different categories of products in the market and aware us about new ideas and services launched in the market. As TV is a medium that has all the moving characters, with their accurate color image and high quality of sounds, it feels as if we can see that person and everything happening in real on those big screens.

We get to know about different brands on television, and hence can search them on internet later. Women who are housewives need some entertainment in their lives too. So these serials attract them a lot. But on the same hand, they watch it so much that it creates an impact on their mind and they start behaving the same as what is shown in the serials. They start believing in what is shown to them.

Finally, TV can be used in many important aspects of everyday. People get entertainment from films, songs, serials or cartoons. People want to be educationally aware these days. TV shows include documentaries or educational programs on the Discovery channel or History TV 18, or through cultural programs.

TV tells us about the happenings around the world, locations, other cultures, other people, other languages and gives us new ideas. It introduces us to knowledge for the world that how one can survive. As we all have seen, television offers us a large amount of valuable programs and content which serves many different purposes of our daily lives style. TV provides us many other types of programs with interesting channels or broad content, as well as, it also serves to our needs in entertainment and knowledge.

TV is the best medium today for providing information. It spreads positive as well as negative information depending on people's understanding, educates the society, and increases people's awareness in every walk of life. TV will continue to have a strong influence on everyone for the years to come.

43

THE MODERN GIRL

"She is a dreamer, thinker, a doer, a maker". Those days are gone when girls used to hide behind the four walls of a house. They did not know about anything except household chores and managing household accounts. From their childhood only, they were taught how to cook food and manage a house. Therefore, they were not sent to school to study and were married at the age of 16 or 18 because it was believed that girls are meant to work at home.

But with a great change, a simple girl can be called by the name 'Modern Girl'. The modern girl is no longer shy, docile and a homely person that she used to be.

In the modern era, girls are not only educated but also they are employed in big companies, banks, stores, schools or hospitals and earn for her family and herself. Their ideas are now inclined to be wholly professional and independent and stand at par with the males whether it is about fashion, ambitions, or professionalism.

Girls these days are more conscious about their personality, the way they look, their dressing style and much more. They are more attracted towards the latest fashion trends, for their charming appearance and looks and for they go to beauty salons, go for skin-therapy, do yoga and gym, eat nutritious food and do dieting.

They wish to spend their quality time more in parties and concerts, pubs and discs and wish to dine in a posh hotel or restaurant.

A modern girl is one who is brought up and educated like anybody in a town or city. There is no difference between her and a boy except in their sex. She gets education in the schools and colleges at par with a boy. She has no fear or shyness which was to be found in the girls of one generation ago. She goes to the school on bicycle. She rides on a scooter and also drives a car. She plays badminton or lawn-tennis and mixes freely with boys on a level of equality and humanity.

A modern girl is, therefore, rightly conscious of her significance as a part of society. She competes with boys in every field and walk of life. She has achieved self-confidence through her education and freedom. She aspires to be an I.A.S. or I.F.S. officer. There are, at present, many women magistrates, officers and professors.

A modern girl is, like the boys, very particular in dress. She insists upon wearing dresses of the latest fashion. The reason for this is that she wants to look as smart as the boys. She wants to make an impression on others.

A typically modern girl is working side by side with the boys. She cycles, swims, takes part in sports and games like the boys. She even takes part in politics. She does not mind mixing freely with the boys. She is dynamic, managing her household chores as well as professional work exceptionally well.

Every change has both good and bad sides. The modern girl and her life are full of rather excessive freedom. She has westernized herself completely and is losing the peace of her mind managing both, home and work. Excess of everything is harmful and so is this westernization. Adopting modernity is not at all bad but forgetting your cultural values is not at all modern. She must follow the path chosen by the great women of the earlier generation. She must not forget the Indian way of life and the great tradition of nobility and sacrifice which many Indian women have made.

44

DIWALI

India is known as the land of festivals due to its cultural diversities, beliefs, and religious faiths among people of different religions. Diwali is the biggest and most celebrated festival of Hindus all over India. It is known as the festival of lights and is celebrated 20 days after the festival of Dussehra in the month of October and November. It is mainly celebrated to depict the classic truth of victory of good over evil.

There is a detailed history behind the celebration of Diwali. According to the Hindu mythology, Lord Rama who was the incarnation of God Vishnu, was a great warrior king and ideal son of Dashratha, the king of Ayodhya. Due to the plotting of his stepmother, his father asked him to go for a-fourteen-year exile. Being an obedient son Rama duly agreed to it. His wife Sita and younger brother Lakshman also stood by him and accompanied him to the forest. During the end of their exile Ravana, the mighty king of Lanka, who heard of Sita's beauty abducted her and took her to Lanka. Rama and Lakshman went to Lanka to kill Ravana and to bring back Sita. The two brothers were accompanied by Hanuman, the greatest disciple of Lord Rama and his warriors. Lord Rama defeated the evil Ravana, put an end to the demon, and brought back his wife, Sita. After this victory, Rama, Sita and Lakshman returned to Ayodhya and their people gave them a grand welcome by lighting the whole of Ayodhya with rows of clay lamps and by firing crackers. So, this occasion marks the honour to Rama's victory over Ravana; the victory of Good over Evil.

115

Now-a-days people celebrate Diwali with the same spirit. They clean their houses and get it re-painted before Diwali. They buy and wear new clothes on this day. In the evening people illuminate their homes with rows of small earthen lamps called *diya*, and light candles to eradicate the evil and welcome God and Goddesses. These days people also use electric hangings and row of beautifully decorated bulbs to lighten their homes. Sky lanterns or sky candles are also used to enliven the beauty of homes.

According to the Hindu religious belief, Goddess Lakshmi, the goddess of wealth, pays a visit to each house and bestows her blessing on them. Due to this belief, people light candles and *diyas* at the entrance and leave their doors open to welcome the goddess. People also perform Lakshmi and Ganesh Puja for blessings and bright future and prosperity. People also visit their relatives and friends and exchange gifts and sweets or dry fruits. Children also take a keen interest in this festival. They indulge in making colourful *rangoli* in bursting of crackers and fireworks and also decorating their house. Also, people get together and celebrate it with delicious food accompanied with music and dancing.

This festival has certain disadvantages also, as a result of negligence the people are injured during bursting crackers, also sometimes fire breaks out, which causes much damage to life and property. Also the smoke and noise can cause health issues and increase the pollution levels. Some people also indulge in gambling on this occasion, and suffer heavy loss. People are advised by the government to be careful and also avoid using crackers and instead use sky candles. Still Diwali remains the most cherished and celebrated festival in India. Keeping the festive spirits high, we all should practise pollution free Diwali in order to enjoy the natural beauty of environment.

45
ANNUAL DAY FUNCTION

One of the most amazing and fun loving function of a school is the Annual Day Function where everyone is filled with excitement of watching some new and amazing activities. The main purpose of this function is to disclose annual result of the school with some entertainment and to give away prizes to the winners of these activities and to recognize the students who achieve first position and perform exceptionally well in academics.

Even those students who are not involved in any of the activities are excited to have a no study day in the school. The preparations for the annual day function are so much fun and as I was one of the host for this function I have missed so many classes, stayed after school hours for practicing my script as I had to be perfect.

Finally the function took place on 12th December, 2014 at 11 am. Students were eagerly waiting for the entertainment part. The function took place in the school ground which was beautifully decorated by the whole team to create an impression on the Chief Guest, other guests, and parents. On the arrival of the Chief Guest, the school band started playing the music. He was escorted by a reception committee, including the members of our school, and the principal.

It started with the principal's speech, in which she welcomed our Chief Guest and then give a detailed description of the school results. Finally, the students who secured first rank and performed well in academics were awarded prizes by the school principal and the chief guest. All, including the principal, the teachers and the students were happy and excited. Then the Chief Guest started giving his speech followed by speeches from the Head-Boy and the Head Girl who thanked teachers, the principal for her guidance and teaching and for providing a great platform to shape up their future.

The principal then expresses gratitude on behalf of everyone to the Chief Guest for accepting their invitation and giving away the prizes to all the brilliant students and becoming a part of the annual celebration. The cultural program began after the prizes have been awarded. The ground was decorated with big writings, balloons, banners, handmade decorative materials and lights.

Students participated in various activities like dance, drama and music programs, for which these students had practiced for long hours and so many days. Songs were beautifully sung by the students, the items of dance and drama were presented and one could see the hard work, students had put in for the program.

The function ended with the principal giving thanks to the Chief Guest, students and to all the parents for sparing their valuable time to attend the school function. The program ended with the National Anthem, sung by our school band and everyone stood up for it. Everybody was given refreshments. Parents waited outside for their children with a big smile on their face especially the ones whose children were awarded with so many prizes.

46

CHRISTMAS

Christmas is both a sacred religious holiday and a world-wide cultural and commercial phenomenon, even in a non-Christian country like India. For two millennia, Christians of all sects around the world have been observing it with various traditions that are both religious and secular in nature and sometimes are adopted from European pagan rituals. Christians celebrate Christmas Day as the anniversary of the birth of Jesus Christ of Bethlehem, a spiritual leader and prophet whose teachings form the basis of their religion. Popular customs include exchanging gifts, decorating Christmas trees, attending church, sharing meals with family and friends and, of course, waiting for Santa Claus to arrive. December 25, Christmas Day, has been a federal holiday in the United States since 1870.

Christmas Day is celebrated every year with great joy, happiness and enthusiasm like other festivals throughout the world. It falls every year on 25th of December in the winter season. Christmas Day is celebrated on the anniversary of the Jesus Christ. On 25th of December, Jesus Christ was born to the Joseph (father) and Mary (mother) in the Bethlehem.

All the houses and churches are cleaned, white washed and decorated with lots of colourful lightings, sceneries, candles, flowers, and other decorations. Everyone gets together (whether they are poor or rich) and enjoy this festival with lots of activities. People make a Christmas tree at this day in the middle of their homes or a public square. They decorate it with electric lights, gift items, balloons, colourful flowers, toys and other materials. Christmas tree looks very attractive and beautiful. Nowadays, most Christmas trees are artificial.

People invite their friends, relatives and neighbours to join the celebration in front of the Christmas tree. People get together, dance, sing, distribute gifts, and enjoy eating delicious dinner. The people of Christian faith pray to the one God and confess their sins and sufferings. People sing Christmas carols in the praise of their Lord Jesus. Later they distribute Christmas gifts to their guests and children.

There is a trend of giving Christmas greetings or other beautiful Christmas cards to the friends and relatives too. Everyone takes part in the great celebration of Christmas feast and eat delicious dinner with their family and friends. Children in their homes wait for this day very eagerly as they get lots of gifts and chocolates. Christmas celebration also takes place in schools and colleges a day or two before Christmas when students go to their schools wearing Santa Claus costumes or just a Christmas cap.

People enjoy this festival till late at night by dancing and singing in the party or in the malls and restaurants. It is considered that Jesus (the Son of God) was sent on the earth to save their souls and protect them from their sins and ignorance. People of the Christian religion celebrate this festival of Christmas to remember the great works of Jesus Christ, the savior and give lots of love and respect. It is a public and religious holiday when almost all the government and non-government organizations are closed for the day in Christian nations or countries with a sizable Christian population.

47

DUSSHERA

Dussehra or Vijayadasami is one of the most important festivals of Hindus. It has a vibrant history and has a great significance and influence on Hindus. Dusshera is celebrated for the victory of Lord Rama over the demon, Ravan who was the king of Lanka. It is the day of celebration of victory of good over evil.

Dusshera is celebrated in the month of Ashwin according to Hindu calendar. It is a ten day long festival, first nine days are celebrated as navratris (people worship goddess Durga) and the tenth day is celebrated as Dusshera. It falls twenty days earlier to Diwali in the month of September or October every year.

As described in the historical epics of Hindus, Ravana had abducted Sita, the wife of Lord Rama while they were in fourteen-year exile. Lord Rama fought with Demon Ravana in the battlefield for long ten days to rescue Sita. On this auspicious day, Rama killed Ravana and rescued his wife Sita.

People throughout the country celebrate this auspicious day in their own ways. Many preparations are made for this festival. It is celebrated with great zeal and enthusiasm. Temples are beautifully decorated with lights and flowers. Idols of Lord Rama, Mata Sita, Lord Laxman and Lord Hanuman are beautifully decorated. People also perform various puja on this day in their houses and pray for peace and prosperity.

Every year in several towns and cities, even in metros like Delhi, Rama Lila is organised by local social committee. Ram Lila stars on the first day of Navratris and it is ten days long event. We perform *puja* in morning and in evening; we all are gathered in the Ramlila ground to watch Ram Lila. Rama Lila is a dramatic folk enactment of life of Lord Rama and Mata Sita. In Rama Lila local children took part and they perform with joy and happiness. Every evening we all gather to see this dramatic show. One of my favourite scenes of Ram Lila is when Lord Hanuman sat Lanka on fire with his tail. On the tenth day of Ram Lila, i.e. Dusshera huge paper models or effigies of Ravana, Kumbhkaran and Meghnath prepared and filled firecrackers are fired in an open area in the ground. On a carriage Jhankis of Lord Rama, Mata Sita, Lord Laxman and Lord Hanuman are taken out from temple to the society ground. Children wear monkey dresses. They dance and sing in joy and happiness. Enthusiasm is its peak when lord Rama fired a burning arrow on the effigies and crackers exploded with noise. Ravana, Kumbhkaran and Meghnath go up in flames and evil also goes away with this fire. People shout and chant for the victory of good over evil.

Dusshera teaches us to look forward towards goodness. It symbolises elimination of evil by burning of Ravana. Dusshera creates a faith in good activities and marks a day of happiness, joy, and end of evilness. It inspires all of us to fight against evil spirits and marks the victory of good over evils.

48

HOLI

Holi is a festival of colours and fun. It is the festival of unity and celebration of victory of good over evil. In India Holi is one of the most important festivals. It is celebrated all over India with great joy and enthusiasm every year in the month of March. Vibrating colours of Holi have a great significance of love, joy, and happiness.

In India we celebrate different festivals throughout the year but Holi has a history and has great influence on Hindu mythology. Once upon a time, there was a young prince named Prahalad who was the son of king Hiranayakashyap. Hiranayakashyap was a demon and he did not believe in Lord Vishnu. Hiranayakashyap wanted people and his son to worship him instead of Lord Vishnu but Prahalad was a great devotee of Lord Vishnu and was a great holy spirit.

Therefore, his father decided to kill Prahalad as he was not obeying his orders of stopping the worship of Lord Vishnu. His father called his sister Holika who had a boon that she would never be killed by fire. King Hiranayakashyap, asked Holika to burn Prahalad by taking him in her lap and sat on fire. Unfortunately, instead of Prahalad, Holika was burnt and died due to fire and Lord Vishnnu saved Prahalad.

Therefore, Holi teaches us that every evil spirit has an end. Holi is a beautiful festival that makes people come closer to dear ones, end all the sadness and hateness, and people enjoy the Holi with peace. It is also beginning of harvest season. Therefore, a day before Holi farmers and family members roast some new corns in the fire and share it among friends, relatives and other family members and the people put the ashes of fire on their foreheads for a peaceful year and prosperity. People pray for a healthy and prosperous year.

On the next day people start playing Holi with different colours. People put the gulal on family members, relatives, neighbours, and children. They play Holi with colour water. Children enjoy playing Holi with family members and friends. They play pranks and pour colour water on everybody. Children fill coloured water in balloons and throw on the people who are roaming on the road. Children seek blessing from their elders and from god.

At the time of Holi people enjoy and dance with joy and enthusiasm. They put speakers on terrace, play drum with loud music, and dance with each other. People take blessings from elders so that the coming years would be peaceful and they can be saved from any type of evilness. People meet each other and celebrate their happiness and joy by rubbing colours on each other cheeks. They greet each other and offer different types of sweets. Gujias are specially made on the occasion of Holi and it is served to all the guests.

Holi is a symbolic festival of victory of good over evil. It has a great significance for Hindus and people need to understand the importance of real happiness and peacefulness. Holi gives a message to live life with truth, joy, and peace and to fight against any evil spirits.

49

INDEPENDENCE DAY CELEBRATIONS IN MY TOWN

India got independence on the auspicious day of August 15, 1947. On this day India got liberation from English rulers after their reign of over 200 years. This liberation was achieved by the Indians after a great struggle made by its freedom fighters for about hundred years. The history of India's freedom states that thousands of people sacrificed their lives in the struggle and faced inhuman tortures of the English people.

After a long struggle by the Indians and the efforts of our father of nation Mahatma Gandhi under the banner of Indian National Congress, this liberation was achieved and this day of Independence is celebrated in the memory of our great freedom fighters.

People of our country celebrate this day every year with great zeal and enthusiasm, as it was the red letter day in the history of India. The main program is celebrated at Red Fort in capital of India, Delhi. On this auspicious day the Prime Minister of India hoists the Tricolor flag at Red fort every year. Our first Prime Minister Pandit Jawaharlal Nehru started the celebration of this occasion on August 15, 1947, who had unfurled the tricolor National Flag at the Red Fort in the national capital, New Delhi for the first time.

The tricolor of our Flag represents saffron for courage and sacrifice, white for peace and truth and green for faith and chivalry. The same celebrations are held in every city and towns, schools, universities etc. On this eve the government establishments as well as schools remain closed for the celebration and to remember the sacrifices of our freedom fighters.

Like every year, this year also the Independence Day was celebrated with great zeal and enthusiasm in my town. The Independence Day program was held in the University Hall. The District Magistrate was the Chief Guest of the program. In the morning at 8 a.m. the national flag was hoisted at the University hall. The flag was unfurled by District magistrate. All the honorable dignitaries and the people saluted the flag and sang the National Anthem.

After hoisting the flag cultural program was started, students of various universities and schools participated in the program. Patriotic poems and songs were recited by the students. The school students marched out in a procession through the main streets of the town with a band playing the National Anthem. People enjoyed by flying kites which signifies independence.

At the end of the program District magistrate gave an inspiring speech. Various dignitaries gave a speech on the sacrifices of thousands of freedom fighters (such as Mahatma Gandhi, Bhagat Singh, Netaji Subhash Chandra Bose, Sardar Vallabhbhai Patel, Dr. Rajendra Prasad, Maulana Abul Kalam Azad, Sukhdev, Gopal Krishna Gokhale, Lala Lajpat Rai, Lokmanya Bal Gangadhar Tilak, Chandra Shekhar Azad, etc.) who worked hard to get independence from the British rule.

Independence Day is the day which reminds us of those patriots who fought and suffered to win freedom for us. Independence Day has a great importance in the life of all citizens of our country. We all should always be together to maintain peace and harmony among the people of different castes, creeds, and religions and spread love and peace to enjoy the real independence.

50

JANMASHTAMI

Janmashtami is an annual celebration of the birth of Lord Shri Krishna Vasudev, the eighth incarnation (avatar) of Lord Vishnu. On this day Lord Krishna was born in Mathura city of the present state of Uttar Pradesh in India. Janmashtami is celebrated on the eighth day of Krishna Paksha in Bhadrapada month of Hindu calendar. Krishna was the eighth son of Devaki and Vashudev who were imprisoned by the king Kansa of Mathura at the time of birth. Janmasthami is also known as Ashtami Rohini, Srikrishna Jayanti, Krishnashtami, Saatam Aatham, and Gokulashtami. This is usually celebrated in the month of August or September. Hindus all over the world celebrate Janmashtami with great enthusiasm and joy. On this auspicious day Hindus observe fast and chant shlokas of Bhagwad Gita. It is famous in Maharashtra for Dahi Handi.

Janmasthami is celebrated every year with great joy in our society. The celebrations are started from morning at 10 a.m. onwards. The whole society is decorated and the old women of society sing Bhajans of Lord Krishna in the society park. All the youngsters of society took part in the contest of Dahi Handi with great enthusiasm. People light up their homes and celebrate Krishna's birth in a grand manner. Priests decorate temples with lights and flowers. An idol of baby Krishna is placed on decorated mantapa and is offered foods like Makkan (butter) and Mishri (sugar cubes). The pictures of Krishna's infancy are placed in swings and cradles in temples and homes.

In the evening at 5.30 p.m. I along with my friends visited temple and the queue was so long that it took around one hour to get in the temple. There were small children dressed up as lord Krishna and Radha who were performing dances and acted on the childhood life of Lord Krishna. Like every year, this year also there were professional troupes who were invited to perform Raas Leela in which people enact scenes and events from Krishna's childhood days and adult life as well. People gathered in the temple community hall to watch Raas Leela. One of my favourite scenes was the one in which Lord Krishna was stealing butter from a house and a few women called Gopian were running to punish him. Children took participation in the function organised by the society members. They participated in the singing and dancing competition and performed beautifully on the songs of Lord Krishna. Society head also awarded winners with prizes to motivate them. After the birth of Krishna at 12 a.m. 'Aarti' is performed and Rudra Abhishek in which Lord krishna's idol is made to bath with milk, honey and ganga jal. After that priest offered sweets to lord Krishna and then distributed various types of sweets to the devotees along with sweet buttermilk. The devotees were excited to get Prasad from priest. Enthusiasm was at its peak.

Krishnashtami brings much joy and feeling of unity. One should also try to follow the teachings and advices given by Lord Krishna to lead a happy and successful life. Janamastmi is the celebration of joy, peace, rise of good over evil and we should celebrate it with the spirit of hope, love, and cooperation for each other.

51

PRIZE DISTRIBUTION FUNCTION IN MY SCHOOL

Prize distribution function is one of the most amazing and important functions of a school. In the prize distribution, we all get to know what achievements our school students have made. It is the most memorable event of the institution. It is held after end term examinations at the end of the year.

The prize distribution in our school was held in the last week of January. It was held in the school hall. The school hall was colorful, decorated with flower pots and banners, maps, pictures and paintings hung on the walls. Chairs were arranged for the visitors. The stage was beautifully decorated. The floor was covered with red carpet. All teachers were looking the sitting arrangements. The Director of Education was invited to preside over the function.

The Chief Guest arrived exactly at 12 p.m. Principal with other members of the staff welcomed him very nicely at the gate of the school. Our chief guest was the CEO of Times of India, Mr. Raj Verma. The school band played the national song. He was accompanied by the principal and members of the school committee to the hall.

The function started with a short drama in which the students became actors, ministers, postman, school teachers, manager and much more. The school students also organized some dance performances and acts which the students in the audience and teachers were enjoying.

After that, a beautiful dance performance was presented by small girls with their beautiful dresses on Vande Mataram. After that our principal read the annual report about the progress, examination results and other school activities like dancing, drawing, race, frog jump race, long jump, basketball, football and much more.

The chief guest gave away the prizes. I also won a prize for standing first in the group dance competition. After that the chief guest delivered a short speech in which he told about what steps one should follow to become a successful person in life. I just liked his speech which motivated me a lot. He also praised the school for its brilliant progress. After that there was a short speech by our school principal, in which he asked the students to maintain good image of the school and congratulated them on their success.

The principal thanked the chief guest and students for coming and announced the head boy and head girl of the year and with it their responsibilities towards the institution. The function ended with a melodious song sung by our school band and with it a beautiful and graceful dance performance by Xth standard boys and girls.

52

REPUBLIC DAY CELEBRATIONS

After 100 years of struggle of our freedom fighters and after sacrificing numerous lives of patriots of India, we got freedom from foreign rulers on August 15. After Independence, it was a great task on the shoulders of our national leaders to choose the form of government and run the administration of the country. Our leaders chose the form of Republic type of government, which means the government of the people, for the people and by the people. In this form of government, the people of the country choose their representatives to govern the country by means of elections and by casting their votes for which a constitution is to be formed containing all detailed issues for smooth governance of the country. For writing Indian constitution a team of national leaders headed by Dr. Bhim Rao Ambedkar was formed. The designated team formed our constitution after consulting constitutions of various countries. This constitution of the people, for the people and by the people came into force on 26th January 1950. This day is called Republic day of India. This day is celebrated every year. It is the day on which India became a Sovereign Democratic Republic and had a constitution of its own.

The Republic day is celebrated all over country with the same spirit and enthusiasm. For the last few years the dignitary of other countries are also invited to the celebration of Republic Day. Such celebrations are also made at different capitals of states by the governors who are the representatives of President at state level.

131

The celebrations start by the visit and salutes of Prime Minister at Amar Jawan Jyoti at India Gate. President of India comes on the dice in his royal carriage (buggy) of seven horses along with his guards. The President of India hoists the National Tri-colour flag, as the National Anthem is played and the 21 guns salutes is given by PGB renders the National salute. After hoisting the flag national awards like Ashok Chakra, Kirti Award, and Param Vir Chakra are given by the President to the members of armed forces before the Armed forces start their march past. Medals are awarded to members the armed forces for their bravery and awards to the meritorious and brave children of the country are distributed. The procession starts from Vijay Chowk. In the lawns of India Gate, all three wings of armed forces i.e. Military, Air force and Navy take part in the celebration by marching from Vijay Chowk to Red fort, Chandni Chowk via India Gate, Mahatma Gandhi road, Connaught Palace, and Lahore Gate.

Besides the march of forces, the defence equipments like tanks, guns, ships, aircraft as well as tableaux or *jhankis* from all the states add to the attraction of the marching procession. Tableaux represents a true picture of the life and customs of the people of the respective state showing the existence of 'Unity in Diversity in India'. Folk dances are held. The students of various states perform in their annual republic parade by dancing, singing, and by marching. At the end of event, there is a colourful fly past by the Indian Air Force. A tricolour of saffron, white, and green, the colours of the national flag are showered and the balloons are flown in the sky indicating the symbol of the peace.

On the 29th January, the celebrations end with beating retreat by the bands of all three forces at Vijay Chowk of India Gate.

53

E-LEARNING

E-Learning or electronic-learning basically refers to learning aided by internet technologies. It includes numerous domains – learning theory, computer-aided training, online learning, and, m-learning i.e. learning done through mobile phones.

We live in a fast moving world where one needs to go hand in hand with the technological innovations that take place in it.

"Live as if you were to die tomorrow. Learn as if you were to live forever." Mahatma Gandhi

Learning is the key to succeed in life. Starting from memorising the alphabets to forming phrases and sentences or taking baby steps to learning to run. All these teachings play a vital role in developing an individual mentally as well as physically.

Teachers and parents are the real gurus. They lead us to the path of success but today, internet technologies seem to be surpassing their knowledge. One can find information about any topic on internet now-a-days; they don't need to search for sources elsewhere to gain knowledge. E-learning provides a virtual space on the world wide web for the teachers and students where they can carry on the learning process with applications like video conferencing, slide presentations, videos, etc. Also, it provides them with an extra feature of interactivity in websites like Wikipedia wherein they can modify the content on the basis of their knowledge and it even allows individuals to take online courses from universities in a variety of subjects.

E-learning is an inexpensive and easier mode of learning which helps one can gain handful of information about the topic sitting at home, sometimes even at zero costs. Internet has revolutionized the education sector by breaking geographical barriers in learning with the inclusion of e-learning tools like:

(i)   **Author a POINT lite:** It is a professional authoring tool that helps in creating content and then convert them into power point presentations.

(ii) **CourseLab:** It allows the users to create content in a WYSIWYG programming-free environment.

(iii) **Easy Generator:** It allows its users to make e-learning courses online without knowledge of programming languages like HTML and XML. Its users mainly include the teachers and professors.

(iv) **GLO Maker:** Glow Learning Objects, is an interactive application that provides its users a feature to operate mobile devices for learning.

(v)   **A Tutor:** It basically aims at providing due services to the academic market and includes customised themes and web-based content delivery.

(vi) **Morzino:** It allows its users to create and publish the e-learning content aimed for online teachings or online learning like virtual schools, etc.

There are various other software applications like the ones mentioned above that are available on internet for the ease of students aiming to learn. But, the users must be very cautious while searching for information on the internet. They must be wise enough to relocate or understand authentic and credible data. A lot of websites and applications are fraudulent they only aim at gaining sensitive information of the people. So, one must be very careful. As on one hand where it fulfils the knowledge requirements of people there, on the other it too hinders their mindset and provides unauthentic information. Also, if one wants to get credible and authentic information from internet, they should visit websites like Wikipedia, gaiaeducation.org, worlddpulse.com, etc. In addition e-learning enables its users to understand concepts in a better way by providing the feature of videos.

"Picture says a thousand words."

Thus, one can easily understand technical terms or processes by viewing them and also enhance their practical knowledge.

But, somewhere the technology has also handicapped people's minds. People are reliable on internet for gaining all information. They don't use their brains at all they totally rely on the technologies to gain information. So, it is very essential to utilise the worth of the brains that helped create such technologies.

ICT is another aspect related to e-learning. It includes the information and communication technologies that aid the learning process by making the lessons interactive and interesting using proper imagery and videos for the users. Thus, E-learning has made the learning process easy and fast if utilised effectively and efficiently. It is a big boon to the education sector and to the society as a whole.

54

INDIA'S FIRST BULLET TRAIN

ndian Railways is one of the largest organizations of the government of India, which gives employment to more than 17 lakhs people . In India the first train was run between Mumbai and Thane in 1853.

Indian Railways is the biggest railway system of Asia and the second biggest railway system of the world. However, as of 2015 it does not consist of any line classed as High-Speed Rail (HSR), which allows an operational speed of 200 km/h or more. The current fastest train in India is the Gatimaan Express that runs with a top speed of 160 km/h, with an average speed of above 100 km/hr between Delhi and Agra.

Prior to the 2014 general election, the two major national parties (Bharatiya Janata Party and Indian National Congress) pledged to introduce high-speed rail. The INC planned to connect over million cities of India through high-speed rail, whereas BJP, which won the election, promised to build the Diamond Quadrilateral project, which would connect the cities of Chennai, Delhi, Kolkata, and Mumbai through high-speed rail. The project was confirmed as a project of priority for the new government in the President's speech. The construction of one kilometer of high speed railway track was estimated to cost Rs. 100 – 140 crore which is 10 to 14 times higher than the construction of a normal railway track.

India's Prime Minister Mr Narendra Modi approved the choice of Japan to build India's first high-speed railway. The planned railway would run some 500 kilometers

(310 miles) between Maharashtra capital Mumbai and the western city of Ahmedabad, at a top speed of 320 km/h. Under the Japanese proposal, the construction is expected to begin in 2017 and be completed in 2023. It would cost about 980 billion (US$15 billion) and be financed by a low-interest loan from Japan. India will use the wheel based 300 km/hr HSR technology, instead of new Maglev 600 km/hr technology of the Japan used in Chūō Shinkansen.

The signing of the bullet train agreement between India and Japan has generated rancorous debate in the media and on social media. The question being asked most is: Does India need a bullet train or, is India even ready for one?

According to the agreement, Japan will provide $12 billion to build India's first bullet train between Mumbai and Ahmedabad. The highly concessional loan, at an interest rate of 0.1 percent, to be repaid over 50 years, will have a moratorium for 15 years. Meanwhile, China is conducting feasibility studies for a high-speed link between New Delhi and Chennai. China has offered a long-term loan too, but not as cheaply as provided by Japan.

Prime Minister Narendra Modi has long been a champion of bullet trains for India. Announcing the agreement in front of Japanese Prime Minster Shinzo Abe, a visibly pleased Modi said, "This enterprise will launch a revolution in Indian railways and speed up India's journey into the future. It will become an engine of economic transformation in India."

However, like anything that Prime Minister Modi is personally involved, this has given his detractors another reason to flog his policies. Social media was flooded with all kinds of expert comments: India does not need bullet trains; and bullet trains are only for the rich. One argument claims that this is being done to satisfy one man's enormous ego. So, once more, battle-lines seem drawn according to whether one likes or does not like Modi. There's no middle ground here.

Interestingly, both sides put out figures, unveil statistics, and make strong arguments on whether bullet trains are needed or not. Some sceptics, who have probably done more homework than the others who blindly oppose it just because it is Modi's project, say that the money is better spent developing existing railway infrastructure. It makes more sense to improve railway tracks to enable trains to run faster, rather than spend money on a few trains that go very fast. They are probably right.

The advocates of bullet train also have valid views and support the facilitation of this transport. For instance, the cost of a kilometre of bullet train track is less than that of a metro. Anything new or daring is opposed by some people. Over the years, everything has been criticised for being wasteful expenditure; from the Indian space programme to the Konkan Railway and the Delhi Metro. Even after achieving tremendous success and huge profit, these are still criticised, but it is noticeable to see the difference they have made. The Konkan Railway has become the lifeline of the west coast, ferrying thousands of people and tens of thousands of tonnes of goods every day.

Sometimes, grand projects such as Delhi Metro, the Konkan Railway are not necessarily only about viability, though that should be a primary concern. Designing and executing such complex large projects boosts national confidence and pride. These have changed the way India looks at major public projects from the point of view of timelines, efficiency of operations, cleanliness, or even managing construction on difficult terrain or conditions. Neither, probably, has yet seen the profit. But quick profit is not the aim of public transport projects.

People in Bangalore spend more time commuting from their home to the office than it will take to travel from Mumbai to Ahmedabad on a bullet train. In the 1970s, a train journey from Bangalore to Delhi took three days. When the Karnataka-Kerala Express and Tamil Nadu Express trains were introduced, the journey reduced to 36 hours. Most people couldn't believe it. The things haven't got either faster or safer since then. And that needs to change.

Is there really a good time for a bullet train? Our country is expanding in implementing technological advancement in the railway network in addition to the above means of transport. The studies show that bullet trains spur business and tourism, create jobs, and build economies India is waiting for the running of bullet trains and such other projects for ease of commuting and transportation.

55

DELHI METRO

From bullock carts to horses to cycles to cars, there has been a drift in the automobile sector. Technological advancements in this sector have made travelling easier and comfortable for the people within short span of time. Public transport has also seen a sudden shift from rickshaws to non-ac buses to ac buses to Volvos to the most widely used metro. Metro is one of the most astounding creations of mankind.

The Delhi Metro Rail Corporation was started in the year 1995 and the first intersection on the 'Red line' opened in 2002 with four coaches increasing it to eight coaches in the present scenario. Today, it is the 12th largest metro system in the world both in terms of length and number of stations consisting of about 160 stations including 6 Airport Expresses and has a ridership of an average of 2.867 million people on board daily. Also, the Delhi Metro Rail Corporation has been certified as the first metro rail and rail-based system by the United Nations in the world to get "carbon credits for reducing greenhouse gas emissions" and aiding in minimising the pollution levels in the city by 630,000 tonnes every year.

The Delhi metro provides for its customers the convenience of travelling with comfort and ease. One coach is significantly made for the ladies to travel across places safely and seats are also reserved for senior citizens and physically challenged people in the train. Also, people are provided with three modes of payment for availing the ticket namely, RFID Tokens, Travel cards and Tourist cards. It also provides cloak room facility at various intersections and arrives at regular intervals and therefore, most of the people travel by metro today.

Metros are one of the safest modes of transportation today. It has about 5,200 CCTV cameras installed to cover every nook and corner of the train, Intercoms are provided in each train for emergency communication between the passengers and the train operator; and periodic safety and security drills are carried out at different stations and on trains to ensure vigilance of security agencies in emergency situations. Every station has ATM machines, eating joints and convenience stores in it for the people and it is strictly prohibited to smoke and eat inside the train so as to ensure cleanliness. This makes the Delhi metro the cleanest of all public modes of transportation. Also, people are provided with charging sockets in the metro to charge the batteries of their laptops and mobile phones.

India is developing rapidly both economically and technologically. Delhi Metro is one of the technological and most wondrous innovations of all time. It is not only eco-friendly but also cost effective for the people to travel in. eIt has indeed brought a revolution in the public transportation sector and furthermore, DMRC is looking forward to increase the number of coaches in the train and to improve the safety and security of the passengers.

56

MOBILE PHONES: PROS AND CONS

Mobile phones or cell phones have made revolutionary changes in the field of communication and have shortened the long distances. Today, we can get connected instantly with our friend or relative sitting in any part of the world. Cell phones have become a very important part of our daily lives as most of our work is done through cell phones. Mobile phones have its positives and negatives.

Benefits and Loss of Mobile Phones

In recent years, mobile phones have become popular all over the world. They are dramatically changing the way people contact to each other. It is apparent that mobile phones have had a profound influence on personal lives. However, not all the effects of them have been positive. To begin with, using mobile phones is one of popular methods for people to communicate, do business and entertain. By making a call or watching a video, sending text messages, we are able to keep in touch with others despite long distances. These days, smart phones enable users to entertain, surfing the internet, sending photos or downloading videos and games. According to a research, the number of people accessing the web through mobile phones is over 15% of worldwide. Furthermore, some office applications for mobile phones, for example, Microsoft Office are helping employees do their business more effectively. Many mobile phones allow access to the Internet, which can help a child obtain answers to questions very quickly and easily. This can help with studies and can inform us about daily weather or finding directions to go somewhere for the first time.

Some cell phones are built with tracking devices through which parents or guardians can track the location of their child and ensure if they are safe. Also, cell phones allow parents and children to stay in touch. If a child needs to stay after school and needs a ride, they are able to call their parents and let them know by simply using their cell phone. Cell phones prove very useful in emergency situations when a parent needs to quickly get in touch with their child or vice versa.

Although it is true that people are now getting a number of advantages from mobiles, these communication technologies have several negative impacts. First, using cell phones too much is harmful for health as it can increase the risk of brain cancer. In addition, children are spending a lot of their useful time on chatting or playing games on mobiles. This is time-consuming and affect negatively on their studies. Lacking of face-to-face communication is also the result of using mobiles. Instead of going out or dating to interact with others, many people prefer to stay at home and use their cell phones to connect to others.

Thus, mobile phones have both advantages and disadvantag in our society. They make people's lives and works more convenient. Yet, mobile phones still impact badly on health, consume fruitful time of children and adults. To avoid these problems, each person should manage the time of using mobiles reasonably. Besides, the awareness of the negative effects of mobile phones should be spread through various modes of communication.

57

NON-CONVENTIONAL SOURCES OF ENERGY

Non-conventional sources of energy refer to the renewable and ecologically viable sources of energy that cause no harm to the environment like solar energy, wind energy, biomass energy, ocean energy (tidal energy, wave energy, ocean thermal energy), geothermal energy, nuclear energy etc. These sources are also non-polluting and environment-friendly besides being renewable. According to an estimate India has a non-conventional energy potential of 1,95,000 w. Of this total potential, 31 per cent is provided by solar energy, 30 per cent by ocean geothermal energy, and 26 per cent by bio-mass and 13 per cent by wind energy. If only one-fourth of this potential is exploited, it will save about million tonnes of petroleum per year valued at 2,770 crores.

Sources of Energy

The different sources of energy are explained below:

(i) Bio-energy

This form of energy is obtained from biological system either by direct use of biomass or by converting it into gaseous and liquid fuel. It includes biogas. Bio-energy is of two types – Biogas and Biomass.

(ii) Solar energy

The energy generated from the use of sunlight is called solar energy. In a tropical country like India, the potential of solar energy is unlimited.

(iii) Wind energy

The energy generated from the use of wind is called wind energy. India now has the largest wind power installed capacity in the world which has reached 1870 MW. About 11.8 billion units of electricity have been fed to various state grids from wind power projects. Wind energy is available in plenty in coastal areas and hilly region.

(iv) Tidal energy

Tidal variations in ocean can be used now to produce electricity. Tidal variations of a large range are found to occur in the Gulfs of Cambay and Kutch on the west coast and the estuary of the Ganga on the east coast. Also there is the possibility of development of small scale tidal power in the Sundarbans areas on the East coast.

Another big source of energy, especially in metropolitan cities is the garbage and refuse. Big tanks at Okhla in New Delhi receive human excreta through drain from a particular area. It is recycled in a way to produce gas that is supplied to the nearby area for cooking. It can also be used for lighting the household. The leftover after processing provide rich natural fertilizer. The city garbage in Bombay is supplied to a firm that processes it in a way and ultimately changes the garbage into small coal ingots which are used in place of coal in all manufacturing units. There are a number of such plants in Bombay. All these unconventional sources of energy are free from environmental hazards and are economical too.

Wood has been the most common source of energy since the advent of human beings on the earth. Increase in population meant occupation of land for residential houses. That is how forests started depleting and disappearing too. Since 18th century coal known as black gold was used in place of wood. But the scientists knew that as the industries grew and the population increased, coal reserves may last only for a hundred or two hundred years. The discovery of petrol of course proved a boon.

Sources of energy are limited, so we must use them wisely and in the right manner. Also we must focus on the use of non-conventional sources of energy to avoid any environmental hazard and keep our environment neat and clean. Thus, it is the need of the hour to run and support environment-friendly programmes at government level.

58

POPULATION EXPLOSION

Population explosion refers a huge and drastic increase in the number of people residing in a particular area or region. It is conceived as one of the greatest threats to the development and growth of an economy. Between 1959 and 2000, the world's population has been projected to increase from 2.5 billion to 6.1 billion people and according to United Nations extrapolations, the world population will rise between 7.9 billion and 10.9 billion by the year 2050. The world population has significantly risen only after the 1700s.

The developed countries like U.S.A. and United Kingdom comprise limited population with ample amount of resources in hand. They are rich enough to employ all potential individuals according to their skills leading to growth and development prospects of the nation as a whole whereas, underdeveloped nations like Gambia, Liberia and developing nations like India and China are the worst hit by the problem of population explosion. The number of job opportunities created in the country is not even equal to half of the population residing. India is anticipated to be the world's most populous country by 2022, exceeding China. Today, India accounts for 15% of the world population consisting of 1.25 billion people approximately, whereas the land area comprises only 2.4%. According to 1981 census, population in India was 685 million with about 354 million males and 331 million females.

Population explosion is majorly due to factors like increased birth rate, decreased infant mortality rate, improved life expectancy and ignorance about family planning. It has a widespread impact on the economic and social stability of the economy leading to problems like overpopulation, increase in the level of poverty, illiteracy, unemployment, increasing health problems, increasing environmental problems like pollution and global warming due to extra amounting pressure on the earth.

Population Connection formerly known as Zero Population Growth or ZPG is a non-profit organization in the United States which aims at raising awareness about the population challenges and exponents for enhanced global access to family planning and reproductive health care. Many organisations all around the globe are working in order to control the menace caused by over population. The government of India both at central and state levels have implemented laws and policies in order to curb the problem. Family Planning is an official programme launched in 1952 which aims at acknowledging people about the importance of family planning. The parents were convinced to go in for sterilization after the birth of two children as the contraceptive pills were not always found to be safe and full-proof. The state governments too came forward to help the central government in its bid to attain success in the programme. Cheap contraceptives were distributed in even the remotest villages, sex education was popularized, vasectomy operations were conducted and abortion was legalized. Also, the government is trying to educate the people by initiating RTE (Right To Education) Act that guarantees free and compulsory education for children between 6 and 14 in India under Article 21A of the Indian Constitution.

Thus, in order to control the problem of over population we as citizens of India must control the birth rate and do family planning. This in turn will not only better our lives but will also better the nation as a whole. The activities of the nation in independent India are directed towards providing adequate means of livelihood to an increasing number of people through an incorporated development of all sectors ranging from agriculture to trade to commerce and industries. The schemes adopted and implemented for this purpose cannot materialize unless the population problem is tackled satisfactorily.

59

SUSTAINABLE DEVELOPMENT

Sustainable development refers to the practice of utilising of natural resources in a way, that it can meet the needs and demands of the present as well as future generations without undermining the integrity, stability and beauty of natural biotic systems. In 1987 a report on sustainable development was made by the World Commission on environment and development. Sustainable science studies the concepts of sustainable development and environmental science as a means to overcome the sustainability issues of the economy and its development. The concept of sustainability has three pillars on which it stands namely, economic, ecological and social.

Ecological sustainability is subject to the relationship between humans and their natural, social and built environments. It includes fundamental human needs such as availability and quality of air, water, food and shelter.

Economic sustainability focuses on the optimum utilisation of natural or ecological resources in a way that it doesn't hinder economic growth or development of the nation. It aims to achieve an environmental equilibrium wherein the supply and demand of natural resources are equal i.e. the needs of all the people are fulfilled.

Social sustainability is defined as the ability of a community to develop procedures and structures which not only meet the needs of its current members but also the future generations to maintain a healthy economy. It aims at making a socially stable economy wherein everyone stays together as one.

SDEWES (The International Centre for Sustainable Development of Energy, Water and Environment Systems) is a non-governmental and non-profit organisation that works on overcoming the sustainability issues all around the globe. The SDEWES Index is the benchmark initiative in the area of sustainable development. It is an effort created to analyse the performance of cities on the basis of energy, water and environment systems. The SDEWES Index consists of 7 dimensions, 35 indicators, and approximately 20 sub-indicators. It is presently functional in 58 cities.

Some of the best known and most extensively used sustainability measures include corporate sustainability reporting, Triple Bottom Line accounting, World Sustainability Society, Circles of Sustainability, and estimates of the quality of sustainability governance for individual countries using the Environmental Sustainability Index and Environmental Performance Index.

The Sustainable Development Goals (SDGs) are the existing synchronized set of seventeen future international development goals that outline the need of the hour explicitly eradicating poverty; providing healthcare facilities; fulfilling food requirements; ensuring education at all levels; achieving gender equality; ensuring availability of water; ensuring access to affordable, reliable, sustainable and modern energy; promoting sustained, inclusive and sustainable economic growth; providing full and productive employment; building resilient infrastructure by fostering innovation; ensuring sustainable consumption and production patterns; protecting, restoring and promoting sustainable use of territorial resources in hand , etc. And according to the data that member countries represented to the United Nations about the accomplishment of their SDGs, Cuba was the only nation in the world in 2006 that met the World Wide Fund for Nature's definition of sustainable development, with an ecological footprint of less than 1.8 hectares per capita and a Human Development Index of over 0.8, 0.855.

The continuous rise in the population across countries is yet another factor that contributes to the problem of sustainability. Thus, it is of utmost importance for the present generations to understand the severity of the issue and overcome any harm caused to the natural environment we live in as we haven't inherited this earth from our forefathers but borrowed it for our children. Earth provides us with all the necessities of life and so, it is our responsibility to maintain stability in the environment by not disturbing its processes otherwise the consequences would disturb our processes of being survive on the earth.

60

DUST STORM

A strong wind which occurs at any time, any place is known as storm. When a storm occurs, the wind consists of dust and dust particles within it, which is usually called a dust storm. A storm usually happens in a desert area or at dry places. It mostly takes place at the time of summers. It is not necessary that storms take place in desert areas only. Delhi is not a dry area like Rajasthan but sometimes in the summers, dust storms occur there.

Storm is just a strong wind blowing at high speed and carrying dirty particles with it. In the desert areas where the dust storm is a regular thing, the storm is so strong that the wind moving at a great speed even moves the sand mountains from one place to another.I have experienced these strong winds once when I visited to Rajasthan and in Delhi too.

In the last summer vacation, in the month of May, when I went to Rajasthan, I had an experience of facing a dust storm. I knew that dust storms occur in deserts but I was unaware that I would be facing it too and so I was caught! I understood that a dust storm was reaching as soon as I saw the weather. The sky was becoming dark, and the clouds were changing its colors. I could feel little dust particles in the air and there was almost complete darkness in the sky. I had hardly reached my hotel when the storm was there in real earnest.

I saw the sky, which changed from normal to dark and there was a lot of dust carried in by the air, and small things like paper bags, leaves etc. started flying here and there. I felt suffocated as I am allergic to dust particles but there was nothing that I could do. The wind was blowing with great speed, and the particles of dust were finding their way inside my eyes. I started thinking why I came out of my hotel. I ran towards the bus stop at the end of the road. At the bus stop, there was another guy who was too protecting himself from this scary dust storm. Till the storm stopped, we began to chat to pass our time.

While the storm was at its peak, more and more people came to the bus stop to protect themselves. The coming bus was not at all visible. Such a dangerous situation! Everybody panicked because the storm was so uncomfortable and could also be destructive to man and material. After fifteen minutes of this scene, the strong wind subsided and there was a loud downpour of rain. This put the dust to settle and the heat to subside. After spending a few minutes at the bus stop, and having my first experience with a dust storm, I went back to the hotel, had dinner as I was very hungry and narrated the whole story to my mom.

61

INTERNET: THE NEW SHOPPING MALL

Online shopping has become one of the most popular activities for shopaholics. It is generating immense craze amongst people.Shopping on internet saves time and people can think before buying, they can buy anything from internet just sitting at home. Shopping done through internet is getting popular among many people and it is been liked by the society. When I shop on internet, I find shopping online is more convenient, approving, instead of going to malls where we have to look in hundreds of shops to find our favourite product which is no doubt time-consuming and wasting energy.

We can shop anything online sitting at our homes. We can find a variety of products and services online! From books to clothes, cosmetics to home appliances, beauty parlour to interior decorator, everything can be found within seconds. We always want to stay in touch with our loved ones whether they are near or far away from us. Online shopping has given people a huge platform of staying connected with people whenever they want to. Whether it's the time of Diwali, or birthdays of our loved ones, we can send gifts to our family and friends with the help of Internet.

Brands like Rado, Armani, Baggit or others are not easily available in small towns but on internet we can quickly type our favourite brand name and then guess what? Of course Shopping! So easy and quick! That's the prime reason of brisk acceptance of home shopping by the society.

It especially involves the youngsters who almost do their purchases through online shopping sitting at home. In today's busy lifestyle, people have no time to go for shopping. Therefore, the option of online shopping suits them the best. It is much easier to shop online. We just need to type the name of product or service and select a brand, and fill details and the product will be delivered at our address within next few days. There is a higher probability of finding better prices and discounts online as compared to shopping from malls as it does not involves the cost of any other intermediaries.

We can shop online whenever we wish too but this is not possible for shopping in malls or markets. Online shopping is available 24*7. We will always be updated by the latest style or trends and thus can become a style icon among our friends and other people. Other advantage of online shopping is their payment options. We can pay through net banking, cash on delivery, debit card, credit card etc.

With many advantages online shopping has some disadvantages and risks as well. The return and exchange policies of these websites and companies are not always trouble free as the options are. One should not shop online if s/he requires the product immediately as it can take many days to get delivered. It also carries the risk of sending a wrong or defective product. Quality is a major issue in home shopping. Another problem is that we always have to compare prices from many other websites lest we pay more. The return of a product is not as easy as it takes so many days and procedures involving bank procedures to return our money. The checking of the company whether it is fraud or not, is another big problem.

Hence, online shopping has equal number of advantages as well as disadvantages. But as we can see, it has become a new trend to shop online and as the internet is a buzz with websites like amazon.com, snapdeal.com, flipkart.com, myntra.com, jabong.com, where we can find our favourite brand, people will definitely shop online and save their time and energy but be careful about all the risk factors also so that it always becomes happy-on-line-shopping for us.

62

MOBILE PHONES AND IPODS- SHOULD THEIR USE BE RESTRICTED?

Mobile phones, Ipods, IPads etc. are the latest instruments of communication. Through them we can communicate or get connected with our friends and relatives in abroad within few seconds. Moreover, many apps like Whatsapp, Twitter etc have made it convenient to send text messages, videos, and sounds over long distances within seconds. This has become possible with the advent of modern technology in communications, i.e. Telecommunication. The term, telecommunications is always used in its plural form as it involves many different technologies. Telecommunication stands for the exchange of information through electronic means over long distances .This technology has played a very important role in sharing information and bringing people much closer. At present the usage of this technology has become essential for mankind. One cannot imagine his or her life without these technologies.

There are some advantages and disadvantages of everything. If we see mobile phones as an advantage, the usage of mobile phones at public places can keep people to stay in with each other. Also, in case of emergency, people can easily and quickly contact each other. Mobile phones nowadays come up with camera and other services like email, entertainment, chatting, video calling, listening to songs and watching videos and so on. Through mobile phones the people can capture pictures of events such as music concerts, wedding celebrations, birthday parties etc. Also, these days, taking selfies of every moment has become a trend. If mobile phones will be banned at public, people won't be able to take selfies and share them with their friends and family on social sites. Moreover, people love to listen to music while travelling, restriction will take their enjoyment away. Cell phones can easily be switched to silent/vibrate mode, this will not distract people due to ringtone of incoming calls or messages.

Mobile phones have some disadvantages also. First, using mobile phones at public places can distract and divert attention of the people nearby. For instance, library is the place where people come to read whatever they wish to but allowance of these cell phones inside the library can easily distract people through ring tones or people talking over the phone. Mobile phone usage at public places like hospitals can easily interfere with the medical treatment which can disturb the patients and the doctors as the hospital environment requires silence. Moreover, talking over the cell phone can increase the sufferings of the patients waiting to see a doctor. Mobiles phones can easily slip from the hand when you are in a crowded place or if anyone pushes you by mistake. Often the environment at shopping malls, stores and other public avenues is very noisy and talking over cell phones will add extra decibel. Moreover, its usage in music galleries or prayer rooms can result in discomfort for others and spoil their entertainment or offerings. And too much usage of cell phones affect the health adversely is the most harmful effect.

To conclude, the above views on advantages and disadvantages of cell phones provide reasonable arguments in favour of both views, however, I personally believe that cell phone should be allowed at public places but with some restrictions so that they can remain in touch with their friends and relatives whenever they want their help or in case of any emergency.

63

THE OZONE LAYER

Ozone layer is at the lowest level of the earth. It serves as a protective shield of the troposphere. It is a layer which protects the earth from harmful ultraviolet radiations from the sun. The ozone layer covers the whole earth and protects it. This layer is with variable extent, less dense near the surface of the earth compared to the height of 30 km. The pollution on the earth has large effect on the ozone layer of the earth. The gases created on the earth reach the stratosphere and cause breaking down of the ozone layer through ultraviolet radiation which causes the liberation of free atoms of chlorine or bromine. The atoms which come out are highly reactive with the ozone and disrupt stratospheric chemistry. The reactions deplete ozone layer. Due to draining of the ozone layer, the earth is exposed to ultraviolet radiation. This kind of radiation causes harmful effects to living beings on the Earth. It affects process of photosynthesis in plants. The level of temperature increases and causes various diseases to the skin like skin cancer, skin burns, breast cancer, eye diseases etc. It also decreases the immunity level in humans.

The substantial increase in the surface temperature of the earth has increased global warming. It is not only harmful to mankind but has reduced crop productivity also and has caused in the increase of sea level.

On the protection of the ozone layer, Vienna Conference in March, 1985 was held. In September 1987 this was followed by the Kyoto Protocol of 1997. The Protocol was planed to phase out the use of chlorofluorocarbon(CFCs) and other ozone depleting substances. The treaty was opened for signature on September 16, 1987, and entered into force on January 1, 1989. After that, it has undergone seven revisions. It is believed that if the international agreement is adhered to, the ozone layer is expected to recover by 2050.

Under this protocol a global fund is established for those developing nations who cannot afford technological costs for alternative chemicals. The Kyoto Protocol is the protocol to the United Nations Framework Convention on Climate Change, aimed at fighting global warming. The Protocol was initially adopted on 11th December, 1997, and entered into force on 16th February, 2005.

As in September 2011, 191 states signed and ratified the protocol. Under the Protocol, 37 countries commit themselves to a reduction of four Greenhouse Gases and two groups of gases (hydro fluorocarbons and per fluorocarbons) produced by them and all member countries.

Apart from these International ramifications, various conferences and programs are also held all over the world regularly to protect the ozone layer. September 16 is declared as the International Day for preservation of ozone by the Montreal Protocol. Thus, if we all turn our careless attitude towards our mother Earth, we can protect the ozone layer and save the existence of mankind on the earth for several coming years.

64

PLASTIC - A BOON OR A BANE

In today's world, plastic has become an important and crucial product of our lifestyle. Plastic was invented for fulfilling the basic needs and wants. It is available in many different varieties - shapes, sizes and thickness. Plastic can be molded in different shapes and sizes. Plastic is useful in many ways as well as is harmful to mankind. Thus, it is a matter of serious concern.

Talking about its advantages, plastic can be said as aboon for human life. Plastic is used as carry bags which helps us to carry many different things. It is used by all the people as it is easily available at very cheap rates. Our needs can't be fulfilled without plastic material. It has become necessity of our lives. Earlier bags were made out of cotton or jute. But with the passage of time, it is not possible to make every carry bag of jute or cotton because of the prices.

Therefore, plastic was invented. The cotton and jute bags were replaced by plastic bags and they look good and are much easier to carry. We can find the plastic everywhere. Plastic bottles, plastic chairs, plastic toys are used by everyone. Even plastic containers have taken its place in our kitchen as they are easy to handle and quick to wash than mud pots. Unbreakable plastic material is used in the making of lots of products and is also used in the manufacturing of various articles like television, tape recorder, computers, cellphones etc.

In our day to day lives we use plastic in the form of pens, boxes and many electrical appliances like tube light holder etc.

But plastic has many disadvantages too. It is very harmful for our health and our life. It can't be removed or destroyed. Plastic is also harmful for soil. It causes soil loses its fertility, if it is buried in the land. Plastic is also harmful for water as water will become polluted and will cause diseases if plastic is dumped into it.

It is also harmful for air, as it causes air pollution when destroyed by burning it. Even after burning, its physical form gets destroyed but it still exists in the gaseous form. It takes the form of some dangerous gases when it is burnt and thereby pollutes the environment. Also, due to it, global warming has been increasing. Plastic is also harmful for human health as it becomes difficult to breath.

On consumption of plastic, innumerable animals, birds and fishes die every year. Thus, it is not only harmful to human beings, but also to animals and other species.We are using plastics even in the places, where its use is not required. If we need to protect our environment we have to check the quantity of plastic generated as it cannot be destroyed.

Plastic should be recycled. Wherever not required, its usage should be stopped. We should cultivate the habit of using cloth bags or paper bags instead of plastic bags because it doesn't create pollution. Instead of using plastic containers, steel containers should be used; instead of dumping water bottles here and there, we should send them for recycling. The usage of plastic cannot be completely stopped but can be lessened. It is boon as well as a bane to mankind.

65

ECO-FRIENDLY LIVING AND SUSTAINABLE DEVELOPMENT

Sustainability is simply everything that we need for our survival and well-being, either directly or indirectly from our environment. It creates and maintains the conditions under which humans and nature can exist in productive harmony, that allow to fulfil social, economic and other requirements of present and future generations.

Environmental sustainability involves making decisions and taking actions to protect natural world, with particular emphasis on preserving the environment to support human life. Environmental sustainability is about making responsible decisions that will reduce your business' negative impact on the environment. It is not simply about reducing the amount of waste you produce or using less energy, but it is concerned with the developing processes that will make the businesses completely sustainable in the future.

Now, businesses are wary of quick fixes and short-term gains. They want to grow in a manner that's mindful of all their stakeholders, including global and local communities, economies, and the environment. In other words, they want to practice business in a more sustainable fashion.

Businesses can cause damage to all areas of the environment. Some of the common environmental concerns include: damaging rainforests and woodlands through agricultural purpose, polluting and over-fishing of oceans, rivers and lakes, polluting the atmosphere through the burning of fossil fuels, damaging prime agricultural and cultivated land through the use of unsustainable farming practices etc.

In the past, most businesses have paid a little concern over the negative impact they have on the environment. Every business needs to consider not only the immediate impact on the environment, but the long term implications as well. For example, when manufacturing a product, you need to look at environmental impact of entire lifecycle of the product i.e. from development to disposal before finalizing your designs.

Many large and small organizations are guilty of significantly polluting the environment and engaging in practices that are simply not sustainable. However, there are now an increasing number of businesses that are committed to reduce their damaging impact and even working towards having a positive influence on environmental sustainability.

Environmental management can help enable companies to make efficient use of energy and material resources, as well as help them implement strict controls on greenhouse gas emissions and other environmental contamination.

Environmentally sustainable businesses may also have a competitive edge when it comes to attracting customers and investors. Modern consumers are aware of social and environmental issues and keep themselves informed about which businesses are acting responsibly in the community. Investors are equally aware of these issues and there is a trend of investing in environmentally sustainable companies. Many countries like Australia have been taking initiatives to support the environmental friendly businesses. The Australian Business Award for Environmental Sustainability recognizes the organizations that implement policies and take initiatives and commitments towards enhancement, preservation and protection of the environment.

Admittedly, the process of changing corporate mind-sets and culture to embrace sustainability can be a challenge for some enterprises. The contemporary idea of sustainable business is, at its heart, merely an extension of principles that underpin value eco-friendly development. After all, maintaining an environment that brings prosperity is imperative for the survival and growth of an organization.

But to achieve authentic sustainability, companies may need to broaden their view of resources that are critical to business. Technology will be an important part of the solution. The key will be to nurture a culture that has discipline, patience, and courage to look beyond short-term solutions and opt for business practices that offer the positive impact and longevity. "The great challenge of the twenty-first century is to raise people everywhere to a decent standard of living while preserving as much of the rest of life as possible."

66

A DOCTOR

A doctor is a very important public servant. He/she is a person who is qualified to treat an ill person. A person who is not physically or mentally fit, is treated by the doctor. A doctor helps them to find a cure to their problems and make a person healthy. We need help from a doctor for many diseases like cold, cough, fever, flue, depression and many more other diseases. The main priority of a doctor is to cure unhealthy persons and treat them well.

A doctor brings happiness for us. He for the treatment of a person provides sweet and bitter medicines or injections so that the person gets well soon.

A doctor is a professional who extends his services to his patients without any bias, selfishness or nervousness, thinking Effects of the disease on self. He works in a hospital or a dispensary. Some doctors have their own clinics while some doctors work in private hospitals where they treat their patients and fulfill the duty to cure them and save their life.

Doctors work to prevent the spread of epidemics and diseases. Every now and then dangerous diseases grab the human beings. It is the doctor who can find cure to such diseases. Sometimes, it may take years of painstaking work and research to find the cure, but ultimately the success is achieved.

Sometimes, the doctor has to work whole day and night attending his serious patients or any major accident case. He always has to treat his patients with a smile. He motivates and encourages a sick person. He is a source of hope and strength.

Even in distress, his duty first lies towards his patient. As a result, Indian doctors are well known for their charitable attitude, dedication, hard work and personal touch. They are in great demand all over the world. Many Indian doctors are working abroad in famous hospitals.

Doctors are working all over the country - in cities, towns, small villages.This has facilitated the doctors to undertake complicated operations and treat critically ill patients with success.

A doctor is given the place of the God. He is a great friend of the sick. His behavior towards his patients is always calm and cool. He never gets irritated or nervous and does his best for the sick. A doctor's life is very hard. He or she does not have much time for sleep or take rest as he has to fulfill his duty of treating his patients. If an emergency comes, he has to come whatever the situation may be. Families have their personal doctors too. They do their routine check up every 1-2 months. Also, if there is any problem, they can call them anytime.

A doctor is a very important person in our life because as long as we are alive, we will suffer from health issues and for that we will need a doctor to cure our problems and make our health good and bring happiness in our life.

67

THE POLICEMAN

In every country, rules and regulations are mandatory to maintain peace and safety of the people. These laws need to be followed by everyone and everywhere but there are some people who do not pay attention to thelaws and breaks them, which is for sure illegal and can sometimes harm a person's life.

Therefore, a policeman, police officer or police agent is a person who is authorized law employee of a police force. He is associated with the task of maintaining peace and harmony, detention of criminals, detecting and taking preventive measures against crimes and criminals, protection and safety of the general public and maintaining public order.

These public safeguards have to take an oath to maintain peace among people and fight against any criminal activity and to protect their country's people. They have the power to arrest people and detain them for sometime for their wrong deeds along with many other duties and powers. It is because of them that our lives and properties are safe. Therefore, he is an important part for smooth running of any society and can be called as ' saviour of the society'

Some officers are also given special training for handling cases and situations which are above the general or normal level. It can be for cases such as child protection, civil law enforcement, women's safety issues, investigating for crimes, rape cases, murders, drug and human trafficking etc.

A policeman can be called as our helping hand. In every country a police officer has a different uniform. For example in India, a police officer wears khaki uniform. You can differentiate policemen by their official symbols. He has the authority to keep a stick and a gun or pistol with him to use in any unlawful situation.

Responsibilities of a police officer vary in different situations. Some common duties of a police officer is to maintain peace and harmony, protection of people and property, listening to people's complaints and queries and taking caring of their safety. A policeman should always be ready for any kind of situations that may arise on the spot. Police are also deployed in an emergency service for providing safety to public at large gatherings, disasters, at the time of elections, festivals etc. They also fight against crimes and criminals using their sharp minds and tight force.

When we at our homes relax and enjoy various festivals and holidays, these policemen are always on their duties round the clock. Though they work in shifts, still a policeman's duty is a tough task whether it is traffic police standing the whole day on polluted roads or the police investigating on a missing child's report. He has to work hard according to the rules and regulations instructed by his head department.

A policeman protects us from wrong deeds and stops people indulge in any anti-social activity. We all look up for him whenever in danger. He is the hero of a society, of a country. It is the moral duty of every citizen to cooperate police in every situation so that the culprits and criminals could be sent behind the bars and the people could lead a peaceful life.

68
THE POSTMAN

The postman is an important public servant. A postman goes from one house to another to deliver messages or important information in the form of letters, telegrams, parcels, money orders and gifts. India has the largest postal network across the world.

A postman is the person who brings bundle of happiness for some while for others he may have heartbreaking news. A postman delivers letters either on cycle or walking door to door. But now-a-days most of them have their own cycle. The postman is a very known face who comes to everybody's house to deliver letters, posts etc. in his khaki uniform. He has a bag with him in which he carries all the letters, parcels, money orders, telegrams and gifts. He is a government servant and works for the Post and Telegraph Department.

Postman's work starts in the morning. He is supposed to go to the post office, sort and collect all the letters and posts of his area, which have to be delivered. One more important step before going out to deliver the letters and posts is to put stamp on all the letters by a postman.

The life of the postman is very hard. While we sit and relax in our homes, he is working for the whole day moving from one house to another, from one locality to another in every type of season or weather. Whether the streets are flooded at the time of rainy season, or it is too cold to go outside in winters, he wades through them so that we get our letters on time as it is his duty. In deserts or forests, terrains or hilly areas or any other hostile places, a postman has to pass through all such places to deliver letters, posts etc. He may lose his life while facing the difficulties in such areas.

Holidays and festivals bring happiness to all of us but it increases the burden of a postman. While we enjoy our holidays he is busy with his works. He does not get much holidays. Despite his hard work, he gets a very low salary and even after this he feels happy to bring home the glad tidings.

A postman is an honest and hardworking person. But some postmen are not sincere in their duties. Their careless acts can put a person in difficulties as some of them do not deliver the letters to their respective addresses or do not put letters in the letter boxes and throw them somewhere else. People have to suffer a lot due to their careless behaviour.

The whole life of a postman is spent from moving door to door and in poverty as his earnings are not that much. He takes care of his family in that small amount only. We all should appreciate and respect the hard work done by a postman. There is little scope for his growth and promotion. Our government should do much to raise the living standard of a postman. We should be kind and sympathetic to him as he carries heavy burden on his shoulders.

69

A HISTORICAL CITY - DELHI

The history of Delhi is steeped in struggles, victories, defeats, frustrations, fears, suspicions, brutality and distrusts. If the people mirror the history of all the aspirations and feelings of a city, there would not be a better example than Delhi.

Delhi is a city with many beautiful and heart throbbing histories of it. Many historical remains are spread all over the city. They have been the silent spectators of the rise and fall of empires. It has been the thrones of many ancient empires, kingdoms and invaders. It was also the center of great Indian movements as well as the capital of Hindu Kingdom and Mughal emperors.

We, Indians are proud to have numerous world heritage sites in the capital of our country. It is a center of power and prestige. It's always fascinating to hear about our emperors, their lifestyles, politics, food and a lot more. Reading and studying history gives a feel of going back in time and re-living those days.

Except a few occasions, Delhi has all along enjoyed a place of pride among the major cities. During the medieval period, it was a big center of power and politics. Even under the British rule, the city enjoyed the same position. The archaeological monuments, buildings, museums and minarets are reflections of its eminent past. The buildings, roads, etc. named after eminent personalities reflect the importance and greatness of the people.

In the earlier times, the city was named as 'Indraprastha' by Pandavas but Shah Jahan founded the present Delhi. This city rose to power and eminence and the rulers who achieved power, made monuments, buildings, temples, mosques, tombs, churches, palaces, etc. in remembrance of their beloved one's or on great and auspicious occasions. These monuments are a great source of information and knowledge on social, political, religious, economic and cultural background of the contemporary society. They contain great architectural beauty, historical value and tremendous visual delight. A visitor gets the feel of history after seeing these monuments.

Such places are a great attraction to the tourists — from within and outside the country. They are good source of foreign exchange earnings.Delhi consists of many historical places such as,Lai Quila, Jama Masjid, Qutub Minar, Humayun Tomb, Iron Pillar, Jantar Mantar, Lotus Temple, etc. In these monuments some are of the ancient or medieval time while the other came into existence in modern times.

The Qutub Minar, built by Qutub bu-Din Aybak, is a historical heritage, and one of the greatest attractions for tourists in Delhi. The Jama Masjid, built by Shah Jahan, is a great historical monument apart from being a place of worship. It is known as one of the biggest mosques in Asia. Its beauty and glory are worth-seeing. This magical and beautiful structure narrates the glorious past.

The Jantar-Mantar is another wonderful creation. Located in the central part of the city, it is a great example of architectural excellence in India. This monument is of great astrological importance. Red Fort is built in red sandstone, it tells us about the great artwork of architectures of those times.

Therefore, the capital of our country is of great historical importance.The monuments reflect our culture, tradition, art and design. Most of them are related to some historical events. The city is a mixture of both ancient and modern legacies. It tells us abouts the lifestyles of emperors, the kind of architecture people liked in those days their lifestyles, economy etc. Thus, the city has great historical and archaeological importance. The monuments symbolize our rich culture and architectural skills and excellence. Delhi, no doubt reflects the beauty of our country and is the heart of our country.

70

A HOT SUMMER DAY

In a hot summer day, the thermometer is showing the highest temperature. The temperature in summer season is hardly bearable even during the early hours of the day. All humans and even animals and other living beings find difficulty to survive in hot days. One cannot go out for shopping, or for work even in the early hours.

The time period between dawn and sunrise is mesmerizing. When the day starts with the sun just about to appear, at that time the climate is cool and calm. The cool and energizing environment and the refreshing breeze soothe our souls and make us feel refreshing. This scene can be imagined so beautifully! The calm and peaceful ambience, with lovely sound of birds appears to be enchanting. The shades in the sky look like a painting drawn on a canvas.

But when the sun rises to its peak, the lovely atmosphere changes and as the day passes on, the temperature too keeps on increasing. The heat becomes intolerable. At noon, the sun is red hot. People avoid going out during this time as they can catch fever or problems like heat stroke. When the sun rises and the heat level increases, the plants and animals also begin to feel the severity of the day. Even animals hid themselves in the shade to avoid the heat of the summer. In villages, buffaloes can be seen neck-deep sunk in ponds and streams. They do so to escape heat. The beautiful colorful flowers which have bloomed soon lose their charm during the day hour.

As the day becomes hotter because of the rise in temperature, it becomes difficult for people, especially for the ones who have to go out for work. For example, farmers, people who go for jobs, street vendors, rickshaw pullers etc. Also, for people who have to travel to the places far away from their homes.

Farmers stop working in the fields. Their crops get destroyed to the excessive heat. Vendors on streets, market places etc cover their stalls with a shed. People try to keep themselves cool, by having lemonade, sitting in air conditioners etc. The sunlight is too harsh for the eyes. One cannot see directly towards the sun. Those who have to go out, cover themselves with *dupattas* or caps. People use sun glasses to cover their faces.

Modern technologies have made summer easier for people. Rooms can be chilled up with the help of air conditioners and fans. We sweat profusely when we are away from the fans or air conditioner. We become wet with sweat within minutes because a little amount of heat becomes unbearable during the summer period.

A large number of people die in summer particularly in northern part of India because of heat stroke. But every season has its pros and cons and has its impact on the environment. The heat in summer season kills harmful bacteria, germs, and mosquitoes which spread several types of diseases. The summers make the surrounding dry and clean. In the evening, people start to come out to enjoy ice creams and cold drinks. They go out to parks for a walk, to feel the fresh and soothing air after in A Hot Summer Day!

71

A JOURNEY BY TRAIN IN WINTER

Journey is always engrossing in everyone's life. It charms our mind, gives us a relaxing feel and makes us happy. Journey turns out to be a relief from our everyday unexciting and boring life. After a journey, we feel fresh and can start our work again with the same enthusiasm.

It also fills our heart with peace and tranquility. During the last winter vacation, I got lucky enough as my parents surprised me with the plan of travelling Dhaka to Rajshahi by train. And as I love train journeys I knew that this one too will be a memorable one. My dad's friend resides there. We generally take bus to travel Rajshahi but this time my parents surprised me by deciding to go there by train.

It was 12th December, 2015. A very special day by two reasons: Firstly, we were going to Rajshahi by train and secondly it was my parents' anniversary. A lot excited I was because of both the reasons. We got up early in the morning, did all the preparation and got on two rickshaws. It took almost half an hour to reach New Delhi Railway Station.

My father bought four tickets from the ticket counter for the 'Ekota Express'. We got into the train and found our seats. I ran and sat beside the window seat as it is my favorite place in a train and how can I miss the golden chance of sitting there. Within a few minutes, the guard blew his whistle and waved his green flag and the train started to move slowly at about 7.30 am.

The train left the platform and gradually it obtained speed and I started waving to the people standing at the platform. It is so much fun! I become a small child whenever I sit in a train. The window was open and I could see outside easily. The train was moving at a great speed and there was a great wrench. As we were crossing Delhi, lots of waste and garbage could be seen. What a shame! As we moved towards the village area, many women's were seen carrying pitchers of water, farmers were seen working in the fields, and young boys and girls were shivering in cold. All these left a permanent impression on my mind.

As it was an intercity train, it did not stop at many stations and was not over-crowded. When it was crossing small stations, it seemed speedier. There were a few hawkers selling boiled eggs, chanachur and betel leaf, bread butter, tea and coffee and fried groundnut etc. We had bread and butter in our breakfast. Later an attendant was ordered to bring tea.

The time passed by. I started reading novels to pass my time and as I love books I was loving it. During the journey, my father showed me the Indian border at hilly station. I was enjoying everything around me. In this way we passed ten hours and at last reached Rajshahi. My uncle was waiting for us there with a car. After coming out of the station, it took only ten minutes to reach us at my uncle's house. We were greeted cordially.

Thus, the train journey came to an end. Though I made the journey last year, the memory of it will remain in my mind and heart forever.

72

AN HOUR AT THE RAILWAY PLATFORM

A railway platform is a very huge place in itself. Whether rich or poor, educated or uneducated, everybody has to wait for the train at the platform. At the railway platform people discuss about various topics like business, household chores, education, fashion sense etc but have you ever discussed about the ambience of a platform? I guess very few of us.

Life at the railway station is fast and quick. It seems like a world in itself. People rush around to check and confirm various things such as arrival and departure of the train, platform number. People are standing at the ticket counter for buying tickets and some at the eatables shop buying various food items and waiting for the train.

Yesterday I went to the New Delhi Railway Station to receive my Massi. What a noise there was on the platform! People were shouting; engines were whistling; carriages were being shunted; and trains were coming in and going out. The announcements were made about the arrival and departure of the trains and if a train is on time or not.

The platform was crowded with hundreds of passengers who seemed to be anxiously waiting for the train. Poor fellows! Little did they know that the train was running behind its time? Big bags scattered all over the platform. One has to walk very carefully otherwise he/she will definitely fall down. So many people, so many bags! Looked like a bag's exhibition.

The station looked like a fort. There was a big waiting hall for third class passengers. It was fitted with benches and electric fans. There were stalls selling so many different kinds of eatables. There were ticket-offices, booking offices, refreshment rooms, book stalls and weight checking machine with glowing bulbs around it. Everybody was checking their weight to pass their time.

There was a long bridge spanning six or seven railway lines. On every platform there were tea stalls and book stalls as people love to wait while reading books and drinking tea. On every platform crowds of passengers were waiting for the train and porters (coolies) in their red dress were carrying passengers' luggage on their heads or luggage barrows.

People seemed to be in a hurry moving from one platform to another in search of the correct one. The announcements were made about the train time schedule, train number, number of coaches, and the train name and which place it is coming from and where it will go next.

Loud sound of laughter, people cracking jokes, and gossiping can be heard as the passengers were waiting for the train or if someone is meeting his beloved after a long time. Once my father told me Mumbai, Kolkata, Chennai have even larger stations than this one.

Noise, luggages, crowd, whatever it is, I love the ambience of a Railway Station whether it is about announcements with that ting-tong sound in the last, or it's about seeing people rushing from here and there. Whether it's about waiting for the train with your friends and family or the excitement when the train arrives with too loud sound of the horn, I feel good and attached to on seeing a Railway Station and platforms with so many trains and passengers.

73

HOCKEY MATCH

"Hockey goals are attained not by strength but by perseverance."

Hockey is the national game of our country. It is played all over the country and is not an expensive game like cricket. Even small village children can be seen playing hockey in an open ground. Our country has been champion at the first place from a long time in the world. Still Pakistan is also counted as one of the champions.

Indian hockey holds high regard all over the world; therefore, director Shimit Amin made a movie on Hockey named Chak De India!, which was released in 2007. Hockey is a game which requires a lot of leg movement. In this game the situation changes very fast. The game can change any minute. The players continue to run fast with no stoppage with the ball test score a goal. Dhyan Chand was an Indian field hockey player, who is considered as one the greatest field hockey players of all time. He is known for his extraordinary goal-scoring feats, in addition to earning three Olympic gold medals in the field of hockey, during an era when India was the most dominant team in Hockey. Also known as 'The Wizard' for his superb ball control, Dhyan Chand played his final international match in 1948, having scored more than 400 goals during his international career. His birthday, i.e. 29th August, is celebrated as National sports day in India.

I find hockey matches so interesting that I never miss watching any of the matches. Last Saturday I witnessed a hockey match which was played at our college sports complex between our college team and the team of Medical College students. Both the teams were evenly attached. Hundreds of students came to watch the match between the two teams.

At 3.30 p.m. the players of both the teams with a referee entered the ground. Mr. Ajay of the Medical College was the referee. He is well known for the impartial decisions. The teams took their assigned positions the moment referee blew the whistle, the game started. The eyes of all the students were on the game following the actions and movements of the players. Their facial expressions could easily tell what was going in the match. The ball was rolling very quickly between the players of the two teams.

In the beginning, it was seen that the game was not very fast but later on as the match proceeded it picked up speed. The players of both the teams were tall enough and looked healthy and active. Each team was playing with full concentration and focus. The players of Medical College were wearing white and blue uniforms. The color of the uniforms worn by our college team was red and white.

After fifteen to twenty minutes the game took its pace. Both the teams were now becoming more and more hostile in their moves to win the game. They were trying their level best to score as much goals as they can. The team of Medical college was for a long time exercising control over our team but they were unable to score a goal. The defenders of our team were very strong. They did not give a single chance to the opposite team to score a goal very easily.

Just before the half time, Sumit, the captain of the Medical College scored a goal in a quick and sudden move. The boys of our college team did not lose their heart. They played fearlessly and patiently. But no goal was made before half time.

After the interval, the game started in an energetic way. The spectators were really enjoying the game and it could be seen from their facial expressions. Now our college team occupied the game. Soon our team scored two goals against their opponents within ten minutes after the game had restarted. The students of our college cheered our team with full power to encourage them.

The players of the Medical college were trying their best to fight back and play a good game. But sadly, they were unable to score any further goal till the end in spite of their best efforts. The spectators praised both the teams by cheering for them and with a big round of applause. At last the game came to an end with our college team winning by two goals to one. The Principal of our College congratulated the players of our team for their brilliant team work.

74

AMITABH BACHCHAN

Popularly known as the angry man of the Indian cinema, Amitabh Bachchan is undoubtedly the super star of Bollywood. He is one of the finest and influential actors till date. In addition, he excels as a writer and singer as well. "It is difficult to 'lie low' with a frame and mane such as mine," he says. Indeed! A man with such a great personality and impactful dialogues hasn't been known since ages. A French director François Truffaut once called him a "one-man industry."

Referred to as Big B or Star of the Millennium, Amitabh Bachchan was born in Allahabad and his father, Harivansh Rai Bachchan was a renowned Hindi poet who named him Inquillab initially but changed it later to Amitabh meaning, "the light that will never die" as per the suggestion of a fellow poet. He completed his higher education from Delhi University and his keen interest in theatre was influenced by her mother, who was offered a role in a feature film but she refused it due to family responsibilities.

Amitabh made his first film debut in the year 1969 as a voice narrator in Mrinal Sen's film, Bhuvan Shome which had won the National Award and the first movie he acted in was his as one of the seven protagonists in the film Saat Hindustani directed by Khwaja Ahmad Abbas. This was just the starting, the actor gained stardom significantly after working in movies like Zanjeer, Abhimaan , Namak Haraam and Sholay. Indian cinema saw an upsurge of a great actor in the industry. He has performed and excelled in almost all film genres starting from action in Agneepath to comedy in Piku to romance in Baghban to Family drama in Kabhe Kabhie.

Bachchan also opened his own production company named as Amitabh Bachchan Corporation, Ltd. (ABCL) in 1996, with a vision of becoming one of the topmost in the industry. ABCL's produced mainstream commercial film and distributed them, production and marketing of television software, audio cassettes and video discs and celebrity and event management were also a part of it. The first film the company produced was Tere Mere Sapne, which did not fare well at the box office. ABCL was also the major sponsor of the 1996 Miss World beauty pageant, Bangalore.

A few of his movies like Mohabbatein, Kabhi Khushi Kabhi Gham and Baghban that were released during the beginning of the 21st century nailed the box office and earned billions and movies like Piku, Paa and Black won hearts of millions of people worldwide. He also received numerous awards for them. The Government of India honoured him with the Padma Shri in 1984, the Padma Bhushan in 2001 and the Padma Vibhushan in 2015 for his contributions to the field of arts. He has also been honoured with the highest civilian award by the Government of France, Knight of the Legion of Honour for his outstanding career in the world of cinema, four National Awards and numerous Film Fare Awards as the best actor and supporting actor. He also did a television show named as 'Kaun Banega Crorepati' (KBC) and made his Hollywood debut in the year 2013 with the movie, The Great Gatsby.

Amitabh Bachchan is the jack of all traits. He has also provided his voice for various movies as a narrator. In 2005, he lent his voice to the Oscar-winning French documentary, March of the Penguins, directed by Luc Jacquet and sang many songs. He was also an active member of Rajya Sabha where he contested elections as a representative and won them too. Even today, at the age of 73, he performs with the same zeal and perfection like before and is worshipped worldwide as an idol for his excellency and perfection as an actor and human being.

75

BHAGAT SINGH

A revolutionary and influential personality in the Indian independence movement, Bhagat Singh was a prominent freedom fighter. He was born on 28th September 1907 at Banga, Jaranwala Tehsil, Lyallpur district, Punjab, British India (present-day Pakistan) into a Jat Punjabi Sikh family which had been involved in the independence struggles against the British Raj. Kishan Singh, Bhagat Singh's father had been released from jail at the time of his birth and his uncle, Sardar Ajit Singh was a great freedom fighter who had set up Indian Patriot's Association. His grandfather, Arjun Singh chased Swami Dayananda Saraswati's Hindu reformist movement, Arya Samaj. His father and uncles were members of the Ghadar Party, led by Kartar Singh Sarabha and Har Dayal. Thus, Bhagat Singh and his family were true patriots.

Bhagat Singh did his schooling from Dayanand Anglo-Vedic (DAV) High School, an Arya Samaji institution unlike other kids who attended the Khalsa High School in Lahore because his grandfather was reluctant on sending his grandson to a school where the officials showed their loyalty towards the British government. He was merely 12 when the Jalianwalan Bagh massacre took place, which greatly disturbed him. This massacre strengthened his resolve to drive the British out of India.

In 1921, when Mahatma Gandhi called for a non-co-operation movement against the British Rule, Bhagat Singh left his studies and joined the movement. On suspension of this movement after the Chaura Chauri incidence, Bhagat Singh was highly disappointed and his faith in non-voilence weekend. Due to this he concluded that the armed revolution is the only practical way to win freedom for India.

He continued his studies from National College in Lahore, which was founded by Lala Lajpat Rai. In the College called as the centre for revolutionary activities, he found fellow revolutionaries such as Sukhdev and Bhagwati Charan and others. He was involved in various revolutionary activities. He joined hands with Chandra Shekhar Azad and the two formed 'Hindustan Samajvadi Prajatantra Sangha'. He had a keen mind and intellect that made him a leader in many revolutions. In February 1928, when Simon Commission headed by Sir John Simon came to India, it was boycotted by Indians because the committee had no Indians in the deciding committee.

Lala Lajpat Rai, launched the "Simon Go Back" protest and raised black flags to condemn a committee that was to decide freedom and responsibilities of Indians. During the protest Lalaji died after being hurt in a Lathi charge. Bhagat Singh along with Sukhdev and Rajguru, the two other revolutionaries decided to avenge Lalaji's death. Assistant Superintendent Saunders was assassinated by them, mistaking him for Scott, the Deputy Inspector General who had ordered the lathi to be charged on Lalaji.

Bhagat Singh openly opposed the discrimination that was made between the British and Indian prisoners and went against the dual policy of treatment. He even went on hunger strike with fellow prisoners to express resentment. The British were forced to accept the demands and agree to their conditions, after a month of long strike.

Bhagat Singh along with Sukhdev and Rajguru was interrogated by British Authority and were convicted with the murder of J.P. Saunders. Singh was fearless and admitted the murder and even made accusations against the British rule during his trial for the murder. Bhagat Singh was ordered death sentence along with revolutionaries Sukhdev and Rajguru.

On March 23, 1931, all three of them were hanged to death in Lahore. The cremation of Singh alone was done on the banks of Sutlej River in Hussainiwala.

Bhagat Singh is dotingly remembered as "Shaheed-E-Azam" as he infused spirits in the youth to become heroes and not fear anything when struggling for the nation. The courage that he exhibited served as a great influence for other freedom fighters to fight and win the freedom struggle of India. Even though Bhagat didn't believe in purely non-violent ways of achieving freedom, he also opposed terrorism and wanted the masses to marshal the struggle.

76

MOTHER TERESA

The embodiment of benevolence, a Roman Catholic nun, religious sister and missionary Mother Teresa or Anjeze Gonxhe Bojaxiu was born in Skopje (modern Macedonia). She was proudly known as Blessed Teresa of Calcutta and lived in India for most of the life. Mother Teresa considered the day she was baptised as her true birthday i.e. 27th August and 15th August 1928 was the auspicious day when she committed herself to the religious life. She was always ensnared by the stories portraying the life of missionaries of Bengal and then, at the age of 18 she left her home to join Sisters of Loreto. She also went to Ireland to learn English with an aspiration to become a missionary. Later, in 1929, she came to India and started her training in Darjeeling.

Mother Teresa served as a teacher in Calcutta for more than 20 years and she loved her work but, she was concerned about the rising poverty in the area. On 10th September 1946, Teresa experienced what she later expressed as "the call within the call" while travelling by train to the Loreto convent in Darjeeling from Calcutta for her annual retreat. Though no one knew it at the time, Sister Teresa had just become Mother Teresa", as said by an author.Soon Mother Teresa adopted Indian citizenship. She started her missionary work in 1948 from Patna and received crucial medical training in the Holy Family Hospital. Further, she moved to Calcutta and started helping the destitute and poor come out of their pathetic conditions. Her service for the poor had won many hearts.

One of the foundations, made by women "poorest of the poor", Indian officials and even the then Prime Minister Pt. Jawaharlal Nehru recognised her service.

Mother Teresa once said, "By blood, I am Albanian. By citizenship, an Indian. By faith, I am a Catholic nun. As to my calling, I belong to the world. As to my heart, I belong entirely to the Heart of Jesus. She was totally committed to serve to the poor and needy. She converted an old deserted Hindu temple into the Kalighat Home for the Dying, a free sanatorium for the poor which was later renamed by her as Kalighat, the Home of the Pure Heart (Nirmal Hriday). Later, she opened a home for those suffering from Hansen's disease, generally known as leprosy, and called the hospice Shanti Nagar (City of Peace) and in 1955 she opened the Nirmala Shishu Bhavan, the Children's Home of the Immaculate Heart, as a shelter for orphans and dispossessed youth.

The year 1950 saw the upcoming of the missionaries of charity, after mother Teresa received Vatican permission. The purpose was to care for " the naked, the starving, the destitute, the blind, the disabled, the lepers, all those people who felt discarded, abhorrent, uncared within the society. By 2007 the Missionaries of Charity consisted of about 450 brothers and 5,000 sisters globally, operating 600 missions, schools and shelters in 120 countries.

Peace begins with a smile, said Mother Teresa. She received copious honours, including the 1979 Nobel Peace Prize, being beatified as "Blessed Teresa of Calcutta and many more. She was admired worldwide for her charitable works and her service to mankind.

77

NARENDRA MODI

My aim is to reform to transform, says Modi. For countless Indians, Narendra Damodardas Modi is the man of the moment, a heroic figure from Vadnagar, Gujarat, who strengthened Indian trade relationships with numerous neighbouring and foreign countries from being a worker at a teal stall to the Chief Minister of Gujarat for four consecutive terms to being the 15th and current prime minister of India.

Narendra Modi was born on 17th September, 1950 in an oil-presser community, categorised as an Other Backward Class by the government of India. He completed his higher secondary education from his home town, Vadnagar in the year 1967. He was a keen debater and an active theatre artist. It was when he turned eight; he started attending the local shakhas of Rashtriya Swayamsevak Sangh (RSS). He was 12 when he got engaged to a local girl Jashodaben Narendrabhai Modi (present wife) and ran away from home. During the two years that he was away from his home, he visited several ashrams namely, the Belur Math near Kolkata, the Advaita Ashrama in Almora and the Ramakrishna mission in Rajkot. Soon, he returned to his home town and started working in a canteen at the Gujarat State Road Transport Corporation.

After the Indo-Pakistani War of 1971, he started working a full-time pracharak (campaigner) for the RSS and in a very short span of time, Narendra Modi became an RSS Sambhaag Pracharak(regional organiser), and received a degree in Political Science .

During the state of emergency in 1975-76, he wrote a book in Gujarati known as Sangharsh ma Gujarat (The Struggles of Gujarat), reciting events that occurred during the Emergency. Later, he was assigned to BJP (Bharatiya Janata Party) and soon in the year 2001, he took an oath as the Chief Minister of Gujarat following the seats being lost by BJP during by-elections. He served as the Chief Minister for four consecutive terms from 2001 to 2014.

The Gujarat state led by Narendra Modi sustained to be the top-rank Indian state in terms of "economic freedom" - an index that measures governance, growth, citizens' rights and labour and business regulation amongst the country's 20 largest states. Gujarat prospered during his rule in the state. According to a study, Gujarat enshrined India by improving various Human development indicators such as female education and school drop-out rates declined from 20 percent during his rule, and maternal mortality fell by 32 percent during the same period. Also, he enhanced the foreign trade with Gujarat by visiting the foreign countries and meeting their prime ministers. However, a few of the critics did point out to the poverty-stricken population, the nutrition and education problem, etc.

Narendra Modi was sworn in as Prime Minister of India on 26th May 2014 at the Rashtrapati Bhavan. He started a monthly radio program known as "Mann ki Baat" on 3rd October 2014. He revoked 1,159 outdated laws in first two years of his rule as compared to 1,301 such laws revoked by the foregoing governments over a span of 64 years. He also launched the Skill India Mission in 2015 and liberalised FDI in order to welcome more foreign investments into the country. Beti Bachao, Beti Padhao Yojana and Sukanya Samriddhi Account, "Housing for All By 2022" project, Pradhan Mantri Jan Dhan Yojana, Pradhan Mantri Ujjwala Yojana (PMUY), Swachh Bharat Abhiyan, Pradhan Mantri Fasal Bima Yojana, etc. are some of the initiatives taken by him as a stepping stone towards development and growth of the economy.

Narendra Modi was honoured as the Best Chief Minister in a 2007 through a nationwide survey by India Today, ranked him the 15th-most-powerful person in the world in 2014 and the 9th-most-powerful person in the world in 2015 by Forbes magazine. Also, he was recently declared as the best prime minister all over the world by the World Bank. Thus, he has achieved developmental goals and proved to be a great leader for the nation.

78

SACHIN TENDULKAR

Mark Waugh once said, when you play against Tendulkar, "You almost want to see him get a few runs just to see him bat."

.Sachin Ramesh Tendulkar proudly referred to as "Master Blaster" of cricket is a former Indian cricketer and captain, widely regarded as one of the greatest batsmen of all time and the 'God of cricket'. He started playing the sport at the tender age of eleven and presently he holds an unimaginable record of scoring 34,357 runs in 664 international cricket matches. He is the only player to have scored one hundred international centuries, the first batsman who scored a double century in a One Day International and is also the holder of the record for the number of runs in both ODI and Test cricket, the only player to have completed more than 30,000 runs in international cricket.

Sachin Tendulkar was born on 24th April 1973 in a Maharashtrian family and his father, Ramesh Tendulkar was a well-known novelist. He kept his son's name after his favourite music director, Sachin Dev Burman. During initial years of his childhood, Sachin was interested in Tennis and used to idolise John McEnroe. Later, his elder brother Ajit introduced him to cricket and his coach, Ramakant Achrekar in the year 1984 grew Sachin's interest for cricket. He had become a child prodigy in his school and nearby cricket circles. Finally, in 1987 he was selected to represent Bombay for Ranjhi Trophy. This is where his professional cricketing career took a flight and

195

touched the sky. He was only 23 when he got selected as the captain of Indian cricket team. But his two tenures weren't very successful. The third tenure did wonders for him; he won the man of the series award. During his cricketing career, India won the 2011 World Cup after a wait of 28 years and after winning the cup, Sachin commented that "Winning the World Cup is the proudest moment of my life. ... I couldn't control my tears of joy."

Sachin had lots of ups and downs during his cricketing journey, but his performance remained consistent throughout. In April 2012, he accepted the Rajya Sabha (the upper house of the parliament) nomination proposed by the President of India and became the first active sportsperson and cricketer to have been nominated. With so much fame and applause, he never left his humanity. He sponsors 200 unfortunate children every year through Apnalaya, a Mumbai-based NGO associated with his mother-in-law, Annabel Mehta.

Sachin has been honoured with numerous recognitions and awards during his journey. He won the Arjuna Award by the Government of India in recognition of his outstanding achievement in sports in 1994, Rajiv Gandhi Khel Ratna, India's highest honour given for achievement in sports, Maharashtra Bhushan Award, Maharashtra State's highest Civilian Award, Padma Vibhushan, India's second highest civilian award in 2008 and Bharat Ratna, India's highest civilian award in 2014. Anil Kumble said it would be "tough to see an Indian (ODI) team list without Tendulkar's name in it". One could not have imagined Indian cricket team without Sachin Tendulkar in it. But, on 10th October 2013 Tendulkar announced that he would retire from all cricket.

Sachin Tendulkar is truly an inspiration for all the Indians. He has not only excelled in the sport of cricket and won numerous awards but also done great works for the unfortunate children and women. He is praised by people all over the world and is the subject of various famous books like Sachin: The Story of the World's Greatest Batsman by Gulu Ezekiel, Sachin Tendulkar opus, Sachin Tendulkar – Masterful by Peter Murray, Ashish Shukla. If Cricket is a Religion, Sachin is God by Vijay Santhanam, Shyam Balasubramanian etc.

79

ALBERT EINSTEIN: THE GREATEST SCIENTIST OF ALL TIME

Once we accept our limits, we go beyond them: Albert Einstein

Albert Einstein was born in a Jewish family as the first child of Hermann and Pauline Einstein in Ulm, Germany on March 14, 1879. He grew up in a secular middle class family, his father being a salesman and his mother a housewife. In November 1881 after two years of Albert's birth, his sister Maria – called Maja was born.

After a short time span, the whole family except Einstein went to Milan. Albert attended his elementary school and subsequently Luitpold grammar school. He was not a born scientist. He was not a genius since his childhood. He was an average child whose interest aroused to develop science and mathematics at an early stage. He did not like grammar classes as it required discipline and learning. When he turned 15, he left school without any degree and followed his family to Milan. Einstein applied to the Swiss Federal Polytechnic School in Zurich, Switzerland but lacking the high school diploma he failed almost every entrance exam but scoring very excellent marks in mathematics and physics he was admitted to the school. He further attended school in Aarau (Switzerland) from 1895 to 1896 and successfully graduated at the age of 17 in the year 1896. His ambition was to obtain the diploma of a subject teacher for mathematics and physics.

He moved to Bern, Switzerland where he was given work at the Patent Office as a clerk and things improved and hard times vanished. In his leisure time he worked in the area of theoretical physics. In 1905 he published several of his important scientific works and papers and the year was termed as Einstein's miracle year. One of them deals with the ground-breaking special theory of relativity. Another work contains the most famous formula of the world $E = mc^2$. This formula states that matter can be converted into energy. In this mathematical equation, E stands for energy, m for mass and c for the speed of the light in a vacuum (ca. 300,000 km/s).

In 1903 he married his college mate MilevaMaric. In 1909 he became professor for theoretical physics at the University of Zurich. After that time he was given a professorship in Prague and then again in Zurich. In 1914 Einstein was called to Berlin to work there scientifically. In the same year World War I broke out.

From 1909 to 1916 Albert Einstein worked on the general theory of relativity. After this theory was proven right in an experiment in 1919 (deflection of light by the sun's gravitational field) Einstein became famous overnight. He received invitations and honors from all over the world. There was no magazine which did not report about him and praise his work to the skies. For the year 1921 he received the Nobel Prize for Physics.

After realizing the political situation of Nazi, Germany Einstein left the country in December 1932 and from 1933 Einstein and his family lived in Princeton, USA. At the "Institute for Advanced Study" he found ideal working conditions. Because of his fear that Germany was working on atomic bombs and there continuous efforts to get hold of nuclear weapons forced him to write a letter to Franklin D. Roosevelt, the president of the United States of America, to tell him about the possibility of atomic weapons. In 1946 he proposed a world government in which he saw the only way to achieve continuous peace.

Einstein spent the last years of his life reclusively in Princeton. Until his last breath he worked on a new theory, the unified field theory, which however was not successful. Albert Einstein died at the age of 76 on April 18, 1955.

Albert Einstein is widely regarded as the father of modern physics. For those of us old enough to have seen him in person, listen to him speaking in public or on the radio, and read his writings when they were current, these memories are precious and unforgotten. In addition to being a great theoretical physicist he was looked upon as a philosopher and statesman. His cognitive interests and profound observations extended widely into the other sciences and the social aspects of human undertake. In the 21st century he remains one of the most influential and iconic thinkers of all time.

80

AMARTYA SEN

"It is important to reclaim for humanity the ground that has been taken from it by various arbitrarily narrow formulations of the demands of rationality." - Amartya Sen

An Indian economist, Amartya Sen was born on November 3, 1933 who is famous for his contributions in the field of economics and for the welfare of society and for his interests in solving the problems of the poorest members of society. Amartya was born to a Bengali family in Shantiniketan, West Bengal. Rabindranath Tagore is said to have given his name "Amartya" which means immortal.

He is the son of Amita Sen and Ashutosh Sen who was a Professor of Chemistry at Dhaka University. He completed his schooling from Dhaka, then for his further studies moved to Presidency College which was considered a reputable college of Calcutta where he appeared as the most renowned student in the year1953. He completed his Ph.D. in Economics from Trinity College, Cambridge.

After completing his Ph.D., Sen became a professor at the Massachusetts Institute of Technology. He was also a visiting Professor at UC-Berkeley, Stanford, and Cornell.

He also taught economics at the University of Calcutta and the Delhi School of Economics where he worked from 1961 to 1972, a period considered to be a Golden Period in the history of DSE. From the year 1977 to 1986 he was a professor at the University of Oxford and in 1986, he joined Harvard as a Thomas W. Lamont University Professor of Economics.

Amartya is recognized as "The Conscience and the Mother Teresa of Economics" for his effort in famine, human development theory, the underlying mechanisms of poverty and gender inequality.

He was the recipient of the Nobel Memorial Prize in Economic Sciences for his contribution in the year 1988. In 2012, he helped in the formation of United Nations Development Index. Amartya was the first non-American who was awarded with the National Humanities award.

He is currently working as a professor at the Thomas W. Lamont University and is teaching Economics and Philosophy at Harvard University.

His name was included in the list of "100 most influential persons in the world", in the Time Magazine 2010 edition. People love reading his books! Therefore, for over 40 years his books have been translated into more than 30 languages.

His works in the field of economics have had a remarkable influence in the formulation of the Human Development Report, published by the United Nations. This annual publication ranks countries on a variety of economic and social indicators and it owes much to the contributions made by Sen.

Various governments and international organizations working for the problem of food crises have been influenced by Sen's work. His visibility inspired policy makers to pay heightened attention to those suffering but also to find ways to replace the lost income of the poor through public-works projects, and to maintain stable prices for food.

A vibrant defender of political freedom, he thinks that famines should not occur in functioning democracies because their leaders must be more responsible and responsive to the demands of the citizens. For more economic growth to be achieved in our country, he argued, social reforms, such as enhancement in education and public health, must precede economic reform. Although after spending much of his life outside his native India, his work has always talked on the issues of poverty of India and other important issues and other developing nations and how to overcome these problems. He has always given his best for his nation.

81

DR. B R AMBEDKAR

Dr. Bhimrao Ramji Ambedkar, popularly known as Babasaheb Ambedkar, was one of the architects of the Indian Constitution. A well-known politician, an influential jurist, and a leader who spent his life to eradicate social evils like untouchability, caste restrictions put in all his efforts to fight for the rights of the dalits and other socially backward classes. Ambedkar was appointed as the first law minister in the cabinet of Pt. Jawaharlal Nehru.

Born to Bhimabai on 14th April 1891 in Madhya Pradesh, Ambedkar was the fourteenth child of his parents. He was a victim of caste discrimination as he belonged to the Hindu Mahar caste, which was viewed as "untouchable" by the upper class. Due to this, Ambedkar faced discriminations from every corner of the society. He got admission easily due to his father working in army but discrimination and humiliation haunted Ambedkar even at the Army school, run by British government. Fearing social outcry, the teachers would segregate the students of lower class from that of Brahmins and other upper classes. The untouchable students were often asked by the teacher to sit outside the class.

Shifting to Satara did not help as the change of school did not change the fate of young Bhimrao. Discrimination haunted him wherever he went. In 1908, Ambedkar got the opportunity to study at the Elphinstone College. Clearing all the exams successfully Ambedkar obtained a scholarship of twenty five rupees a month from the Gayakwad ruler of Baroda, Sayaji Rao III which he decided to use it for his higher studies in the USA. Political Science and Economics were the subjects in which he graduated from the Bombay University in 1912.

After his return, Ambedkar was appointed as the Defense secretary to the King of Baroda. Humiliation for being an 'Untouchable' followed him even there. The former Bombay Governor, Lord Sydenham helped Ambedkar to procure a job as a professor of political economy at the Sydenham College of Commerce and Economics in Bombay. In 1920, he went to England to continue his further at his own expenses. He was awarded with the honor of D.Sc by the London University. To study economics he spent few months at the University of Bonn, Germany. On 8th June, 1927, he was awarded a Doctorate by the University of Columbia.

After returning to India, Bhimrao Ambedkar made a decision to fight against the caste discrimination that almost disintegrated the nation. Ambedkar put forward his thought of a separate electoral system for the Untouchables and lower caste people. He also observed that reservation should be given to *Dalits* and other religious communities.

Ambedkar started searching ways to reach to the people and make them understand the drawbacks of the prevailing social evils. He started a newspaper called "Mooknayaka" (leader of the silent). It is believed that after hearing his speech at a rally, Shahu IV, an influential ruler of Kolhapur dined with the leader. The incident also created a huge turmoil in the socio-political arena of the country.

1936 was the year when Ambedkar founded the Independent Labor Party. In the year 1937, his party won 15 seats in the elections to the Central Legislative Assembly. Ambedkar supervised the transformation of his political party into the All India Scheduled Castes Federation, although it did not perform well in the elections held in 1946 for the Constituent Assembly of India. Ambedkar raised objections to the decision of Congress and Mahatma Gandhi to call the untouchable community as Harijans. He believed that the members of untouchable community are no different than the other members of the society.

Ambedkar was appointed on the Defense Advisory Committee and the Viceroy's Executive Council as Minister for Labour. His reputation as a scholar led to his appointment as free India's first, law minister. Ambedkar was appointed as the chairman of the constitution drafting committee. He was also a noted scholar and eminent jurist. Ambedkar highlighted on the construction of a virtual bridge between the classes of the society. He believed that there was an urgent need to fill the difference among the classes to maintain the unity of the country.

In 1950, Ambedkar traveled to Sri Lanka to attend a convention of Buddhist scholars and monks and after his return he decided to write a book on Buddhism and this resulted in his conversion into Buddhism. The speeches of Ambedkar involved the Hindu rituals and caste division. He was the founder of the Bharatiya Bauddha Mahasabha (BBM).

On October 14th, 1956 Ambedkar organized a public ceremony to convert around five lakh of his supporters into Buddhism. Ambedkar traveled to Kathmandu to attend the Fourth World Buddhist Conference. He completed his final manuscript, "The Buddha or Karl Marx" on December 2,1956. After his death on 6th December,1956, his book "The Buddha and His Dhamma" was published. Since, Ambedkar adopted the Buddhism as his religion, a Buddhist-style cremation was organized for him. The ceremony was attended by hundreds of thousands of supporters, activists and admirers. He was posthumously awarded the Bharat Ratna, India's highest civilian honour in 1990. It is rightly said by him- "The sovereignty of scriptures of all religions must come to an end if we want to have a united integrated modern India."

82

MAHATMA GANDHI

"The duty of motherhood requires qualities which man does not possess........

The Art of bringing up the infants of the race is her special and sole prerogative. Without her care the race must become extinct....."

Mahatma Gandhi, the man who advocated non-violence and stood for secularism, was born on October 2nd, 1896 in Porbandar, Gujarat. He did many great things throughout his life. He was born in a well-to-do tradesmen family. Despite being illiterate, his mother had common sense and religious devotion in her, which created a great impact on Gandhi.

He was a regular student in his school times but was not a book worm or sports person. He was a shy kind of student with no leadership quality in him. After the death of his father, he wanted to have a simple life. Therefore, for higher studies he went to England to study law and he became a barrister. There he got involved with the Vegetarian Society and was once asked to translate the Hindu Bhagavad Gita. This created a sense of pride in his heart for Indian scriptures. He also realized the importance of humility and forgiveness.

Gandhi returned to India after completing his degree in law; soon after he went to South Africa for practice. In South Africa, Gandhi faced racial discrimination and injustice often faced by Indians. These events were a turning point in Gandhi's life: they shaped his social activism and awakened him to social injustice. It was in

South Africa that he experimented his first campaign as civil disobedience. His ideas and protests took shape, and the concept of Satyagraha matured during the struggle.

After 21 years in South Africa, Gandhi returned to India in 1915. He became the leader of the Indian nationalist movement campaigning for home rule or Swaraj. In 1919 he started a non-violent and peaceful movement and Hindu-Muslim unity, removal of untouchability and usage of Swadeshi (domestic) goods were his life's goals.

Gandhi dedicated his life to his country and to the wider purpose of discovering truth, Satya. Gandhi's life, ideas and works are of great importance to all those who want a better life for mankind. The political scenario of the world has changed dramatically since his time. The importance of moral and ethical issues raised by him remains central to the future of individuals and nations. He is an inspiration for everyone. We can always learn from his teachings, morals and values. He always wanted everyone to remember the age old saying, "In spite of death, life persists, and in spite of hatred, love persists." Rabindranath Tagore addressed him as 'Mahatma' and the latter called the poet "Gurudev'. Subhash Chandra Bose had called him the 'Father of the Nation' in his message on Hind Azad Radio.

Mahatma Gandhi became a prominent Indian political leader who campaigned for Indian independence. He employed non-violent principles and peaceful disobedience. He was murdered in 1948, shortly after achieving his life goal of Indian independence. His awful death resulted in the heartbreaks of the entire nation. But the whole world still loves and respects him and celebrates 2nd October, his birthday as Gandhi Jayanti which is a National Holiday in India and follow the path he showed.

83

MARRY KOM – A WORLD CLASS BOXER

"To be a successful boxer one must also have a strong heart. Some women are physically strong but fail when it comes to having a strong heart. One also must have the zeal and the right fighting spirit. We work harder than men and are determined to fight with all our strength to make our nation proud. God has given me the talent and it's only because of sheer grit and hard work that I have made it so far." – Marry Kom

India is setting a mark by its performance in the world sports and is talking about boxing which was seen as a male sport, a woman has totally changed the meaning of boxing. A sportswoman who has made Indians and the country proud with her glorious achievements, Mary Kom, the only Indian woman boxer headed exceptionally well and qualified in the 2012 Summer Olympics where she won a Bronze Medal. She is a five-time world amateur boxing champion. Surprisingly, she is peaceful and philosophical about all her achievements.

Known to millions as Mary Kom, her full name is Mangte Chungneijang Mary Kom, an Indian boxer who was born on March 1, 1983. She belongs to the Kom tribal community of Manipur. She was presented with the World Boxing championship title five times and is the only woman boxer in the world to have won a medal in each of the six world championships she participated in.

Born in Kangathei, Manipur, to Mangte Tonpa Kom and Mangte Akham Kom, Mary wrapped up her eight years of education in Moirang and went to Imphal for her ninth and tenth standards. Unfortunately, she could not pass her examinations. Under this situation, she decided to quit school and give her examination from NIOS. She finished her graduation from Churachandpur college. Although she was not a very bright student academically, she did not give up on life. Not everyone is good at studies; some are good at sports or in other activities.

Mary Kom's interest in athletics started to develop when she was young and the success of Dingko Singh, an Indian boxer of Manipur, set her passion on fire and pitched her to enhance her boxing skills and to become a professional boxer. Each one of us have a role model in our life, who we want to become like. Their great achievements in life, their hard work inspire us to take the path they took and this is the same what Mary Kom did. In 2000, she began her training under M Narjit Singh, Manipur State Boxing Coach.

Mary Kom hid her passion and interest from her family as boxing is not considered suitable for women but her family got to know about her interest through a newspaper when she won the Manipur State Boxing championship in 2000. She is an inspiration for everyone especially for the youth of our country who can learn a lot from Mary Kom. Youngsters are afraid to follow their dreams. They always fear rejections from the society. Success can never materialize from fear. To become a successful person one needs to become confident and determined. If you are sure about your goals and your abilities, no one can stop you from taking up the challenges and achieving your goals.

Mary Kom commenced her boxing career at the age of 18 at the international level, which is considered old by several standards. However, she did not lose hope.C

S Lewis, a famous poet and novelist, once said, "You are never too old to set another goal or to dream a new dream". In order to achieve your goals and to see your dreams becoming real, passion, hard work and dedication are necessary; age is not a criterion. Mary Kom proved to the world that age is nothing but a number. Her passion and her dedication to succeed in the world of boxing won her many medals, including a bronze medal in 2012 Olympics.

For her contribution to sports, the Indian government presented her with a number of awards, including the Arjuna Award in 2003, Padmashree in 2006 and Padma Bhushan in 2013. Today, Mary Kom is happily married and has two sons. Her attainment is remarkable, which is why Sanjay Leela Bhansali, an praised film director, made a decision to cast a movie on Mary Kom's life so that thousands of children and adults will get inspired by Mary Kom to excel not only in sports but in any field they are interested in. Today her success is an example for all to see and learn from! Of course, there is more to know about Mary Kom than just professional success. She also teaches boxing to underprivileged youngsters for free. "People used to say that boxing is for men and not for women and I thought I will show them some day. I promised myself and I proved myself' – Marry Kom. If Mary Kom can, why can't one who is confident and determined to achieve the goal set by him/her?

84

NELSON MANDELA

If you can unlock people's potential to become better, then you are a leader. A person who's actions, inspires others to dream more, learn more, do more and, become more is the best example of a leader.

One of the great leaders who had the above qualities fulfilled in him is the former South African president, Nelson Rolihlahla Mandela. Commonly known as Nelson Mandela, he was born in 1918 to a tribal chief of Tembu - Henry Mandela. In the year 1944 he was married to Evelyn Ntoko Mase (a nurse) and after 12 years he had a divorce. After 2 years, in 1958 he married Nomzamo Winnie Madikizela who was a political activist and social worker, and divorced her too. He married the third time with Graca Machel, a lawyer by profession in 1998. From his first marriage he had three children, his two sons Thembi (deceased) and Makgatho, and a daughter Makaziwe. And from his second marriage he had two daughters Zenani and Zindziswa.

Mandela was the first in his family to complete his primary education at a local missionary school. He completed his Bachelor's degree from the University of South Africa (UNISA) through correspondence in 1941 and later in 1942 he pursued his law degree at the University of Witwatersrand, where he got involved in the movement or fight against the racial discrimination and forged key relationships with Black and White activists.

During 1940s and 1950s he joined the African National Congress and rose rapidly through the ANC hierarchy because of which he was frequently subject to detention, police harassments, and banning. The ANC certainly began to intentionally devise a public legend around. Mandela himself took pains to ensure the media images matched the messages, his comrades.

Mandela's political experiences emerged when he was enrolled to the University College (Fort Hare) where he worked to obtain a Bachelor of degree in Fine Arts. During his course, he got elected as the Student's Representative Council of the student political organization. He was expelled for participating in a protest in the campus (ANC archive). Because of this, he left to Johannesburg where he finally obtained his degree in BA. In 1942, he joined the African National Congress, during World War II. Nelson formed a group with other members of the ANC under the leadership of a colleague, Anton Lembede. The main goal of the group was to change the African National Congress into a mass movement.

Mandela performed a major role in many political undertakes, many anti-apartheid movements such as the Program of Action, a policy based initiative that was founded on the principles of non-violent "civil disobedience, boycott, strike, and non-co-operation".

ANC was outlawed in 1960. In 1962 Mandela was sentenced for five years of imprisonment for travel without valid travel documents while leaving South Africa and stimulating Africans to strike. Two years later during his detention in 1964, he was charged with mutiny and was sentenced to life imprisonment for giving four-and-a-half hours of speech criticizing apartheid which is memorable.

Mandela spent twenty-seven consecutive years of his life in detention. For 18 years (1964 - 1982) he was held on Robben Island. In1982 he was moved to Pollsmoor Prison, Cape Town, and in 1988 he was again moved to Victor Verster Prison, in Paarl, till 1990.

From 1985 onwards he started rejecting several offers of "conditional" release which would have imposed limitations on his political activities. His imprisonment improved his political status which resulted in worldwide campaign to release him.

In the 1990s, Mandela led the ANC in its discussions with governing National Party and many other South African political organizations to end discrimination on the grounds of race. The whole thing earned Mandela The Nobel Peace Prize in December 1993.

ANC won the National Elections of South Africa in the year 1994 and Mandela was sworn in as the President of the country. He established the Truth and Reconciliation Commission to inquire into human rights and violations committed by both opponents and supporters of apartheid between 1960 and 1994. He also received numerous international honorary degrees, a doctorate degree from the Open University of Cape Town in 2004 and another honorary degree in 2005 from Amherst College situated in New York.

This great man died on 9th December, 2013 from a lung infection. Nelson Mandela is considered as a rebellious leader with the ability to empower and motivate others using his strong regard for consensus and the democratic process."Let freedom reign. The sun never set on so glorious a human achievement "- Nelson Mandela. In the year 2009, 18th July was declared as 'Nelson Mandela International Day'.

85

SUBHASH CHANDRA BOSE

Subhash Chandra Bose, popularly known as "Netaji", was one of the greatest active, freedom fighters and patriots of his time, who was born at Cuttack, Orissa on January 23, 1897 to Janakinath Bose and Prabhavati Devi. Janakinath was a famous lawyer whereas Prabhavati Devi was religious and believed in God. Subhash Chandra was an excellent student from his childhood and did well in his matriculation examination.

Bose completed his graduation from Presidency College, Kolkata. Then he went to England in September 1919 for higher studies. He got selected for the Indian Civil Service but without completing his training he returned to India to join the fight for India's freedom.

The Jallianwala Bagh mass slaughter and suppression and oppression of the Britishers had deep impact on *netaji*. He wanted to make India free from such injustice and cruelty. Under the deep influence of Mahatma Gandhi, he joined the Indian National Congress. Impressed by Deshbandhu Chittaranjan Das, he began to regard him as his political guru and guide.

Subhash Chandra was elected as the President of the Indian National Congress in the year 1938 and was elected for the same in 1939 also. In this moment he thought to form his own party named the Forward Block in 1939 itself because of his differences with Mahatma Gandhi and other Congress leaders. Bose launched an all-India anti-British Campaign in September, 1939 and was arrested in July, 1940. He reached Malaya and established Indian

National Army (INA) or Azad Hind Fauz by enlisting Indian Prisoners of War. His visit to Japan in June, 1943 was to have support of the Japanese government in the freedom struggle of India. On October 21, 1943, he became the commander of the Indian National Army in Singapore and began his military struggle against the British. He also established the Provisional Government of Free India there. In December, 1943 he occupied Andaman and Nicobar Islands.

In December 1944 the Indian National Army crossed the Burma-India Border and reached Kohima and then Imphal.

"Delhi Chalo" (March towards Delhi) became the battle cry of the Indian National Army and they were soon across the Indian border in Manipur but then the bombing of Hiroshima and Nagasaki took place and the surrender of the Japanese army changed the whole course of events and forced him to withdraw and call off the war. Therefore, he decided to return to Tokyo to decide his further course of action, but unfortunately, his plane crashed near Taipei and he achieved martyrdom at the young age of 48 years. It is believed that he lost his life in a plane-crash on August 18, 1945 at the Taihoku airport, Formosa. But the country took the news of his death with disbelief and still there are thousands and thousands of Indians who believe that he is alive.

Before his withdrawal from the eastern borders of India due to unavoidable circumstances, he had actually occupied and freed more than 1500 sq. miles of the Indian Territory from the British. He had many close associates like Ras Bihari Bose, Shahnawaz Khan etc. Besides Chittaranjan Das, he was also influenced by Bal Gangadhar Tilak.

Bose was a great adventurer as well. His military exploits, unmatched patriotism and exemplary bravery have made him a role model for the young men and women of India. He still lives in the hearts of all Indians and is an example as a leading light and source of inspiration. He would have given a new phase and turn to our political and social life with his dynamic personality and high sense of patriotism.

Subhash Chandra was one of the greatest freedom fighters and patriots and the Pride of Bengal. He was a legend of his lifetime as a great leader, fiery orator and an organizer. He was sent to prison eleven times during 1920 – 1941. Thus, his contribution is no less than other freedom fighters. He was, he is and he will be alive in the hearts of Indians forever. "By freedom I mean all-round freedom, i.e. freedom for individuals as well as for the society; freedom for the rich as well as for the poor; freedom for men as well as for women; freedom for all individuals and for all classes of the society."

86

RABINDRANATH TAGORE: THE EXCLUSIVE GEM OF INDIA

"Clouds come floating into my life, no longer to carry rain or usher storm, but to add color to my sunset sky." — Rabindranath Tagore, *Stray Birds*

Rabindranath Tagore, a sobriquet Gurudev, was a Bengali man of wide ranging knowledge and learning who reshaped his region's literature and music. Tagore, popularly known as Gurudev, was born to Maharishi Devendranath and Sharda Devi on May 8, 1861 in Kolkata. He was member of a well known family of thinkers, reformers, social and cultural leaders and intellectuals.

Tagore was a person of great principles of humanism. He was also a well known painter, patriot, poet, playwright, novelist, story-teller, philosopher, and educationist. Being a cultural ambassador of India, he gave voice to the country and became a source in spreading the knowledge of Indian culture around the entire world. Tagore was not a school going lover. Though he began to write from his early age, his love for his country pushed him to write poems, songs and stories about different aspects of Indian culture and society. A talented, energetic and a wise man whose every word and every touch was magical and enriched.

His words spread warmth and magic and restored mental and moral spirit of the people. His writing proved path-breaking and rebellious. He felt tortured, had pain and sorrow after the Jallianwala Bagh tragedy which took place on 13th April, 1999 in Amritsar and in which General

Dyer and his soldiers killed hundreds of innocent civilians and wounded thousands of people. The incident flustered Tagore so much that he could not sleep when he heard about the incident. He decided to reject and give up his knighthood as a protest and immediately drafted a letter to Viceroy. And what he wrote to him was , "The time has come when pledges of honor make our shame glaring in their incongruous context of humiliation and I, for my part, wish to stand shorn of all special distinctions, by the side of my countrymen, who for their so-called insignificance are liable to suffer humiliation not tit for human beings."

Tagore neither decided the way nor he had powers to fight for India's freedom but his feelings for his nation and a true patriotism were his biggest powers. He was the man with so many qualities inside him. He was a poet, a philosopher and a visionary and voice of the people of the country. He was a great nationalist but his patriotism ultimately merged suitably into internationalism.

Tagore did not like divisions, boundaries and discrimination on the basis of territory, geography, race etc and was against it. He trusted in the oneness of life and god and its expression. Tagore did every possible thing to bring the people from across the world close to each another through his message of love, brotherhood, peace and poetry.

He spread warm radiations like the sun of universal love and harmony by the means of his work and poetry. Nationalism is essential; it is good and healthy for the country; and its people but to a certain limit only. After the limit has been reached, it's neither enough nor desirable.

His words for his country were "My country that is forever India, the country of my forefathers, the country of my children, my country has given me life and strength." And again, "I shall be born in India again. With all her poverty, misery and wretchedness, I love India best." He did not give it a stop and continued his job to embrace the whole mankind.

On 13th November, 1913 he was honored with Nobel Prize for literature, for his beautiful and lyrical collection of poems called Gitanjali (a bouquet of flowers). He was the first Indian who was awarded with Nobel Prize. Gitanjali was published in 1910. His compositions also involved Puravi, the Evening Songs and the Morning Songs and writings on many subjects — social, political, cultural, religious, moral etc.

Tagore wrote Manasi in 1890, which had social and political poems stamped with the mark of his early genius and art. He was a pure Bengali writer whose work involved the life, land and the people of Bengal.

One of his story entitled Galpaguccha sketches the poverty, illiteracy and backwardness of the people very well and effectively. His other well known poetry collections include Sonar Tari, Chitra, Kalpana and Naivedya. His plays include Chitrangda and Malini, Gora, Raja and Rani, Binodini and Nauka Dubai are his novels.

A great educationist who founded a unique university called Shantiniketan (abode of peace). He once said "Deliverance is not for me in renunciation, I feel the embrace of freedom in thousand bonds of delight."

The voice of the country, a man who spread warmth and light, a true patriot, a great son of India, a great bard and lover of nature died on 7th August, 1941 in Kolkata, a few years before India's independence in 1947. He was the man behind the National Anthem of India "Jana Gana Mana." Truly, whatever his genius touched turned into gold and immortality.

87

DISASTER MANAGEMENT

Disasters can be man-made or natural. Man-made disasters are the catastrophes that occur due to human interferences like fire, terrorism, etc. whereas natural disasters are naturally occurring hazardous phenomenon like earthquakes, tsunamis, floods and hurricanes. These calamities cause a lot of damage to the properties, mankind and wildlife. Millions of people lose their lives during such disasters. Thus, there is an urgent need to mitigate the risks related to these calamities. Disaster management of emergency is defined as the planning and making of strategies and tactics that help communities minimise the vulnerability to the hazards and help cope with any such unwanted occurrence.

A recent discovery of the World Disaster Reports found out that the disasters have increased in frequency and intensity over the last few decades. Individuals are becoming more and more susceptible to all types of disasters, including earthquake, flood, cyclones, landslides, droughts, accidents, plane crash, forests fire, etc. and with the technological advancements and progress; the force of disasters is also changing and becoming stronger. Of all the disasters, floods are the most frequent followed by wind storms, droughts and earthquakes. But droughts are the deadliest of all disasters accounting for 48 per cent of all deaths from natural disasters. The highest numbers of people die from disasters in Asia. India, China and Bangladesh are the worst affected countries by flood.

India, due to its vast geographical and climatic differences, is a disaster prone country. Long coastline, snow-clad high peaks, high mountain ranges, the perennial rivers in the north all combine to aggravate it. India having only two per cent the total geographical area has to support 16 per cent of total world population. Naturally, there is a tremendous pressure on natural resources due to which disasters can frequently occur. India has faced a number of disasters, ranging from flood, earthquakes, cyclones, tsunami, drought, landslides. A few recent disasters faced by India include Uttar Kashi earthquake in UP in 1991, Later earthquake in Maharashtra in 1993, Chama earthquake in Gujarat, super cyclone in Orissa in 1999, Buhl earthquake in Gujarat in 2001, Tsunami in 2004 and Mumbai-Gujarat flood in 2005. Besides, India has a bad experience of technology-related tragedy in the form of gas tragedy in Bhopal in 1984. India also faced the problem of Plague in Gujarat.

The UNDA with Government of India has jointly prepared an action plan for cities and towns vulnerable to earthquakes. It is required that a monitoring mechanism should be set up in disaster prone areas and frequent checks should be done.

The Central Government has a facilitating role. It, with proper coordination with various ministries, extends all required support and helps to the states, namely defence services, air dropping, rescuing, searching, transport of relief goods, availability of rail and ferry services, health personnel and medical support, etc.

Disaster is a state subject in India; it is, therefore, the responsibility of the state to provide every kind of support and assistance to the victim. In the State, the Relief Commissioner or Disaster Management Secretary is the specific authority responsible for handling and management of the disaster.In 1999 a high powered Committee on Disaster Management was set up by the Government of

India to look into the existing disaster management system in the country and to suggest measures to improve it. Besides, a Calamity Relief Fund has been constituted with contribution in ratio 3: 1 between the Centre and the respective State Government. The Eleventh Finance Commission has recommended nearly Rs. 11,000 crore for the period spread over five years, while the Twelfth Finance Commission has also recommended a Rs 23,000 crore assistance for the states.

Rehabilitation is an integral part of disaster management. When disasters occur, administrative measures are terribly inadequate and perhaps this is the most difficult period for a victim. The role of administration does not end with end of disasters. In fact its efforts and commitments get more complex. It requires proper coordination among various agencies. In this context it is very important to note that disasters are non-routine events that require non-routine response. Government should not rely on normal procedures to implement appropriate responses – the rescue teams need to learn special skills, technologies and attitudes in dealing with disasters. Emergency planning should made to prevent emergencies from occurring, and failing that, should extend a good action plan to mitigate the results and effects of any emergencies or disasters. It is a great challenge for society across castes, creeds, communities and countries. Disaster Management has assumed great importance in recent times. To handle the situation efficiently, we need to be well-equipped with latest technologies. It cannot avert the situation, but can mitigate its impacts.

88

EARTHQUAKE

Earthquakes are one of the most annihilating and destructing phenomenon that occur as a result of natural process of the earth. Quakes are the noticeable shaking of the earth's surface, which are caused due to unexpected liberation of energy stored in rocks, from the crust; creating what is known as seismic waves.

Earthquakes are usually measured using seismometers and Richter scale whereas the magnitude is measured using the Mercalli intensity scale. Earthquakes of magnitude 3 or less are considered to be weak and indiscernible but earthquakes with magnitude 7 or over potentially cause a lot of damage. The 1960 Chilean earthquake of magnitude 9.5 on the Richter scale is the largest one that has been recorded till date. After it, the 2004 Indian Ocean earthquake is also one of the deadliest quakes that lead to tsunami and took millions of lives.

Research says that about 5, 00,000 earthquakes occur every year but, only about 1,00,000 of the major ones can be felt , the minor ones go unfelt. Minor earthquakes constantly occur throughout the world in places like California, New Zealand, Japan, India, Nepal, Mexico, Turkey etc. Also, geologists claim that global warming is one of the significant reasons for the increase in number of earthquakes.

In India, approximately 38 cities and many states are classified as high risk zones namely, Mumbai, Chennai, Srinagar, Andaman and Nicobar islands, Jammu and Kashmir, Himachal Pradesh, Uttarakhand and Madhya Pradesh, etc. The Himalayas and northern India are particularly shaky ground due to historical reasons, thus the area sees a lot of temblors, one significant being the 2005 Pakistan quake that took about 80,000 lives. About 60 percent of India is exposed to quakes.

Earthquakes cause a lot of destruction to mankind and wildlife. It leads to shaking and demolishing of buildings and other firm structures and ground rupture. Tremors also result in landslides and avalanches due to volcanic activity and wildfires, fires caused by damaged electrical powers or gas lines, soil liquefaction causing many buildings to sink, tsunami and floods due to overflow of water reaching the land.

Invention of newer scientific methods have made possible for the scientists or seismologists to predict the time and place where the earthquake might occur. In fact, earthquake warning systems have also been developed that help in notifying people throughout the world about the occurrence of earthquakes in their areas.

Earthquakes are hazardous natural calamities. These cannot be prevented but, its after-effects can surely be minimised. Thus, in order to minimise the damage caused by earthquakes the government has initiated various schemes and emergency management strategies to mitigate risks. Also, the builders are advised to construct earthquake proof structures as a precautionary measure. Delhi Metro is one of the significant structures that are totally earthquake proof. Individuals are usually advised to hide under the table, move away from densely populated areas, come out the building at once and avoid using lift and stand by the poles during earthquakes. The earthquake engineering also helps anticipate the impact of quakes on buildings and other rigid structures to reduce the risk of damage. Earthquake insurance provides the building's owners protection against losses during tremors.

Thus, by adopting the safety measures, one can evade from the hazardous consequences caused by earthquake.

89

WHEN THE GOING GETS TOUGH, THE TOUGH GETS GOING

When the going gets tough, the tough gets going. This saying originally said by Joseph P. Kennedy, father of former president John F. Kennedy, is very motivational to people all over the world. Its tricky play on words and its motivational tone make it a very interesting quote to look at in depth and to explain exactly what it means.

It is endlessly quoted by football coaches, salesman, and other motivators. "The going" means the situation, "gets tough" means becomes difficult, "the tough" means the people who are strong or enduring, and "get going" means to become fully engaged to meet the challenge. Thus the meaning of the phrase "when the going gets tough, the tough get going" is when the situation becomes difficult, the strong will work harder to meet the challenge.

What does it mean to be tough? A tough person is someone who can survive through hard times. The tough persons overcome adversity and make it through and come out better than they were before. This quote does not mean flee from the situation which is not what strong people do. The strong people persevere through hard situations. The interesting thing about this quote is that the last two words, "get going" can be interpreted in two ways: It can be thought of as in get working to overcome the problem or it could mean flee the situation. It was truly said in the context of persevering through the hard situations. What does perseverance mean. Persevering means a person gets through the situations no matter how hard the situation is. It means they don't give up in any ups and down of life.

Its reference can be taken from a lot of texts like it is used in Animal House in famous Bluto's "Big Speech". It is used in The Lion King II: Simba's Pride by Timon during the battle between the Pridelanders and the Outsiders. Also, it is used in the song "Memo to my son" by Randy Newman, along with a similar figure of speech: A winner never quits, a quitter never wins.

In life we must persevere constantly to go through any hard situation. Only then we will be winner. To avoid any situation is not the solution to the problem but it may lead to another big problem or difficulty. Thus the quote "When the going gets tough, the tough gets going" is rightly said.

90

A RAILWAY ACCIDENT

Nowadays, people have lost self control. They are forgetting their limits. They are always in a hurry to reach the destination or at the place of their work. In the haste, they don't care about the norms and rules and regulations set by the Railways. That's why the incidences of accidents are reported daily. The accidents occur due to human negligence or due to intentional effort made a terrorist. Not a single day passes without an accident. Whether they are road-accidents or they are train accidents or air-crashes, they for sure take place in every corner of the world. And the main reason for these accidents is carelessness of human.

Our daily newspapers carry news about these accidents that have taken place in any part of the country. Several news channels on television showcase full coverage of such accidents. We get sympathized on seeing people connected with these accidents crying for their beloved ones and for their kith and kin who have been killed or injured in these accidents. But one can truly realize the loss of such incidents, when one becomes the victim himself.

One day I was travelling by Rajdhani Express from Bhatinda to Delhi. I started from Patna at 6.20 a.m. The train was overcrowded and there was a great rush. Everyone seemed to be in a hurry. All were looking for their seats. I too was in search of a suitable place and luckily I got it soon.

The train started at its exact time. Everything was OK and all seemed to be in a cheerful mood. The train had hardly travelled three-four kilometers when we suddenly felt terrible movements with booming sound. I fell down upon a woman who was sitting right beside me.

Soon the same happened with another person and so with everyone.The next moment a big wooden box fell upon a woman and she became unconscious. In a few seconds there occurred great disorder. The children started crying and everybody started to panic. There was a fear in everyone's voice and eyes. Men were crying out of pain. I was also wounded. But still I somehow managed to stand up and I realized what was going on and guessed the whole scenario. Other passengers too had guessed about the accident.

And finally it was located that a bomb went off in the general compartment, second coach from the train engine. The tragedy was too shocking and scary to describe. I went out of my senses for a time being and did not know what to do. I saw several passengers were struggling for life because they were injured badly. Several passengers were burnt in that blast and their faces were beyond recognition. We heard cries and moaning from every side. Tears rolled down my eyes.

Some ladies were crying bitterly because their children were killed. A woman lost the company of her husband and was searching for him here and there like a mad person. The scene was really very pathetic and tragic. I could not believe for sometime as it happened with me for the first time.

Soon a Railway Medical Van had rushed to the spot. Along with the accident victims, I too was taken to a nearby Medical camp. Later on, I was discharged after some first aids to my wounds. But the loss was huge: the loss of lives of people. What could be worst in the journey of a train?

I can never forget that accident which took so many lives and smiles of people. But at the same time I am shocked to think that such kind of accidents happen so easily in our country even after the tight security. What kind of security is this? Are we really safe? Should one stop travelling? I do not understand why some people are indulged in terrorist acts. What do they obtain at the loss of innocent lives? Who will find answers to these questions and solve the problem. I pray to God to divert the mind of terrorists into positive direction so that such incidents may not occur forever.

91
ADVERTISEMENTS

Advertising is a business tool used for the promotion of a product, service or even to a particular group of people. Copywriters create advertising matter or tag lines and graphic designers complete it with their artistic skills. Media, TV broadcasts, banners, hoardings, etc. are various means of advertisement and promotion. Advertising plays many different roles in the market. For example, The Marketing role, The Communication role, The Economic role, The Societal role etc.

Another important aspect of advertisement is creativity. Creativity is a very subjective term. Who can really say what is creative, for we all have different opinions on what we individually think is creative. Some people believe creativity is an ingrained concept that you are born with. Other people believe it is a talent that can be learned and taught. It is the ability to generate fresh, unique and appropriate ideas that can be used as solution to communication problem which is very important aspect for a successful advertisement.

Advertisements have become a part of our lives. We cannot live without them; they attract us from all sides. Step out of the house and they stare you from all the corners, promoting products from needles to C.Ds, from cricket bats to gold watches and so on. At home every five minute T.V. programs are interrupted to tell us which toothpaste we should buy, what kind of salt is good for us or even which toy to give to a new-born baby! So many kinds of goods are displayed, so many temptations are presented that the poor consumer does not know what to buy or what to reject.

Advertisements (Ads) are categorized geographically like local ads, regional ads, national ads and international ads. International ads include products of other countries being advertised in a country like India. For example, Playboy, Nike, American Tourist, Arrow, United Colors of Benetton etc all these brands belong to different foreign countries.

Advertisements are a help because they educate us about a new product, its features, how it will benefit us, why it is better from other similar products and a lot more. Without them one would not know what to buy. We will not be able to learn about the merits of a new product or a similar product which has come with advanced technologies and benefits.

It can be anything: a new medicine, a new book, a new school, a new hospital, a new phone or any gadget, the list is endless. Advertisements also lead to competition and better products come in the market. It is a source of awareness about any product, service or idea.

As long as the competition is healthy it is good for consumers, but advertisements have become expensive and cut throat. Take the example of the Cola War. The competition between the Pepsi and Coca-Cola has made them spend crores on ads. Film stars are roped in to make the product popular. It increases the rivalry between the competitors to such an extent that they don't hesitate in crossing their limits to stand first.

Films are advertised with huge posters. Sometimes they prove dangerous for drivers! Some advertisements are in bad taste, which gets down the image of a company while some of them are so attractive that they force the buyers to buy the product whether they need it or not.

Advertisements are a great way to spread awareness but there should be some way to educate the gullible buyer about the quality and price of the product and people should understand that ads are meant only for promotion of sales and publicity of product. They are intended to hurt the feelings or ethics of someone. Thus, ads are a great source of knowing about a product or service and its quality and popularity.

92

AN IDEAL STUDENT

An ideal student is the wealth and future of his nation, hope of his family and pride and glory of his school or college. He is loved by everyone because of his qualities, and great power of knowledge. He knows how to respect his teachers and elders and help his friends or any other person. Such students are the gems of an institution. They are the pillars of a nation as they build a strong nation in terms of education sector. Such students become ideal citizens, politicians, statesmen and leaders.

An ideal student is an all rounder. He takes part in every activity whether it's academic in nature or any sports or cultural activity. He is hard working by nature. He is always punctual to the school or college timings, attends his classes on a regular bases and studies with full heart and dedication and achieves good position in his school or college.

Being disciplined, obedient, respectful to his elders and teachers are some of his good qualities. He always follows the rules and regulations of his educational institution. He has control of behavior in his everyday activities of life. He avoids company of bad boys and focuses on his studies and extra co-curricular activities so that he can make his parents and teachers proud one day.

An ideal student can't be called a bookworm as he takes full interest in games and sports too like he takes in studies. Games and studies go side by side with him. He knows the importance of games and sports, extracurricular activities in his life. He knows that a sound mind lives in a sound body. He considers games an essential part of his education as it refreshes the mind of a student and he can start with his studies plus it also helps in physical as well as mental development.

He always sticks to his right ideals and aims. 'Simple living and high thinking' is the motive of his life. He has a strong moral character. An ideal student possesses the qualities like humble, modest and polite, patience etc.He does not loose hope in difficult situations and face them bravely.

An ideal student is excellent in every field, whether it's about debates, speeches and declamation contests, he takes part in every activity.He is a good speaker and gets home many trophies and medals that make his parents, teachers, institution proud. And these students in future make their country proud by doing a lot good for their country.

Since our country is passing through a difficult period of struggle, it is badly in need of ideal students and citizens. The nation can reach the highest point of glory if our students become ideal and participate in the task of every national reconstruction. An ideal student is the spark of hope, glory and prosperity of his country. The students of today are the future and leaders of tomorrow. The future of the country depends upon them only. Every student should, therefore, try to become an ideal student. An ideal student is ideal in his work, conduct and thought. He works hard and lives for his family and country.

93

AN IDEAL TEACHER

"The dream begins with a teacher who believes in you, who tugs and pushes and leads you to the next plateau, sometimes poking you with a sharp stick called 'truth'."

Dan Rather

The word 'teacher' signifies knowledge that is to be passed on to a learner. The premise that makes a person's life strong and successful is to great extent based on the knowledge he gets from his teacher. Other than our parents, the person who builds our mental skills is our teacher.

In ancient India, the teacher was given respect next to one's parents. Wise men with immeasurable knowledge were called teachers. The students in search of such great teachers used to travel so far to gain education from them. Teachers (in Hinduism and Buddhism, a spiritual person especially one who imparts initiation) were then called Gurus.

As the time changed, people's view towards the education also changed. Education was democratized and was open for all irrespective of caste, class, creed or place of birth. This generated a need for a large number of schools and teachers. In today's time, all kinds of teaches, teaching from pre-primary level to the university level are available. But we have to know who is an ideal teacher?

An ideal teacher has a few special qualities. For example, an ideal teacher is the one who is a hero for his students. A person who has chosen path followed by every student and whose words and actions are like commands

236

to them is an ideal teacher. His words are considered as a truth and whatever he does is considered to be perfect.

An ideal teacher should, therefore, have a good personality and ample knowledge. He should know the art of studying students' minds and understanding their individual problems. Knowledge is ever growing and so an ideal teacher should always prepare his lesions before he enters the class.

An ideal teacher should have confidence in him. His message should be clearly conveyed to his students. Punctuality, good dressing and discipline are some other important qualities of an ideal teacher.

An ideal teacher should consider himself as a parent to his students. Every student is to be looked after and taught with devotion. He should pay attention to a weak student same as he does to a bright one. He should also get involved with the society. His dealings with other teachers and parents should be friendly. Teaching is a professional job. It requires technical skills and knowledge of teaching.

To become an ideal teacher you should fully devote yourself towards teaching and students.Only those with a natural ability to do something can become an ideal teacher. It is said that a nation's future is shaped in its classrooms, and the man who shapes it is the teacher. A school teacher is said to be worth a thousand preachers.

An ideal teacher gets credit and respect for himself, for his school, for society, and for his country. Ideal teachers are honoured in our country with national awards and state awards on the Teachers' Day'.

94

THE CITY I LIVE IN – NEW DELHI

The magical city, New Delhi is loved by everyone. The history of Delhi is filled with struggles, victories, defeats, inspirations, distrust, mysteries and much more. If we go in past time and see what Delhi was, we will find emotions, feelings, family values and a hope or ambition of achieving everything.

Delhi has undergone a structured change since the days of Indraprastha to become an energetic metropolis. After Independence it is the passion and devotion of people that have made Delhi a real metro city. The migrant families who came to settle in Delhi worked hard and established trade here. These are the reasons behind the growth or transformation of Delhi. Their work and trade have big businesses in today's world.

The city is energy converted into culture" these words by Lewis Mumford suits the best for a city like New Delhi. As we enter the gates of New Delhi, the city impresses us with wide roads, big gardens ,heritage sites, multi-storey buildings, dazzling restraunts. Any resident who has been living here for long can tell every single bit about the city with so much enthusiasm.

The face of Delhi has changed beyond imagination. It has become a world class city. Today Delhi is one of the greenest capital cities in the world. The capital boasts of aesthetically appealing foot over-bridges, trendy street lights; sculpted landscaping, world-class transport facilities, glitzy and many more elements of modern infrastructure. Delhi's 'London Eyes', Kingdom of Dreams, Haats of Delhi, Garden of Five Senses, India's Golden Heritage and many more are some important places.

"Dilwalo ki Dillli", "Yeh Dilli hai mere Yaar, Bas Ishq Mohabat Pyaar", these words about Delhi suits its current situation the best.The capital city has undergone a complete change and the development that took place during CWG. With these developments like eco-friendly autos and taxis and the Ho-Ho buses which are widely appreciated by people who witnessed the CWG games. Now we also have a world class airport that has transformed from being an ordinary airport to something big and beautiful. This has been one of the most successful change that has taken place in Delhi. The changing face of Delhi can be seen through this great change.

The protection of Delhi's environment has always been high on the agenda of the environment department of Delhi. The Delhi government has taken essential steps to solve this problem through campaigns like, 'Say No To Plastic Bags', 'Say No To Crackers', playing Holi with natural colors etc. Also the concept of "Green Buildings" was introduced by the government in which natural materials are used in making of the building which are less toxic.

Delhi is a symbol of urban progress rather than urban decay. Apart from all infrastructural and economical development, a change in people's outlook towards everything is seen here. The standard of living and mindsets of people have changed for a good.

Thus, Delhi has the best infrastructure, roads, metro, green, parks, malls, mouth-watering food and a lot more. Being the capital of the country, it has a world class infrastructure and sets an example for every state, every country.

95

THE IMPORTANCE OF EDUCATION

"The only person who is educated is the one who has learnt how to learn and change"   *Oscar Wilde*

Education is the lamp that dispels darkness. "Education is the agent of change. In the contemporary world, it has become a principle aspect of everyone's upbringing. In this millenium, rather than being an aspect of luxury, education has become a necessity. Moreover, it does not only equip us with reading, writing and learning skills but also makes us judicious, improves our thinking skills and how to respond in a situation and leads us towards holistic development.

The Educational sector is a very large sector in India. It includes primary and high schools, under-graduate and post-graduate colleges, B-schools etc. Though a large part of India still falls under rural sector, the educational institutions at that level include small government and private schools and vocational colleges.

What I believe is that education has made the world a better place to live in as it has civilized the uncivilized ones. The people who have chosen the path of education are leading a great successful life and are above the poverty line. Today education has become the need of everybody's life not only because it boosts up self confidence but also results in high intellectual level and raises your general awareness. It is also seen that education has helped in solving many problems like child labor, domestic violence, human trafficking etc. which are posed as immense problems.

Even after eradicating so many problems from a country and serving its people with knowledge so that they can stand on their own feet, it is still believed by some orthodox people that education is nothing but money goes in vain. Education has given a lot to humanity. A child when sent to school for the first time is hesitant, but as the time pass by he changes as education infuses in him the spirit to live a successful and respectful life. Education adds on morals and values to the lives of people. Also, it adds discipline and teaches manners and etiquettes which are very important in a person's life. Moreover, it makes the democratic system more democratic for educated people are aware about their fundamental rights, policies and schemes. Now they can't be deceived by anyone. More and more people are becoming educated hence education helps them in attaining the power of self controlling their lives for their own good.

There are many children who want to learn and gain so much from education but their condition restricts them from doing so. To overcome this problem, the government has introduced many bills and amendments like Right to Education. As per RTE, 25% of the students should be from Economically Weaker Section (EWS). Another example is of "Each one, Teach one" campaign which was introduced successfully.

Education helps us to understand our past and to experience the mistakes made and what needs to be done to improve our present. By working hard and gaining as much knowledge possible we might have a bright and successful future ahead. Hence, one who hasn't been educated hasn't been refined. I strongly believe that India has a great future ahead as long as people and the government remain united to fight against illiteracy and spread education. "Education is the most powerful weapon which you can use to change the world"-Nelson Mandela. Thus, education makes us self reliant, experienced, successful, and the most of it, a good and social human being.

96

EXAMINATION FEVER

"You may never know what results come of your action but if you do nothing no result will come",

Mahatma Gandhi

As the exams approach, students suffer from examination fear and we all know how much students hate examinations. Examinations increase the burden and worries of students. The bugbear of an examination interrupts smooth functioning of a student's life. Games, musical concerts, debates and other extra-curricular activities like mural painting which are favorite activities of all the students have to be stopped during preparing for examinations. Students are not allowed to roam around here and there with friends or pass time except studying. No entertainment at all!

But everything has a reason behind it, probably a good one. Examinations are conducted to test students' knowledge, to check how seriously they have been studying during the classes, to judge what progress and score they have achieved and to regulate whether they have been utilizing or wasting their time. If no examinations were arranged, the merits and demerits of various students could not be judged, nor would the students take any interest in studies and would take exams lightly as it is only the fear of examinations that makes students work hard.

Students know that neglecting their books or studies is of no use as any how they will be exposed in examinations. They know that their results will be conveyed to their parents, and if not good or satisfactory they will land into problem. Also they can't afford to fail as it will create a bad image in front of the society and will give them a feeling of humiliation. All these things develop desire in a student to work hard. Examinations are therefore important for a student and add incentive to work.

But examinations are not a reliable test of the ability of students. A student sometimes is not good at writing but is practically brilliant. A student may memorize portions of the text and if the exam paper is set from the portions a student has prepared from, he will no doubt secure good results, as compared to another student who didn't.

It is also seen that the standard of marking all the papers is different because different examiners mark different papers in different moods. Most educationists now agree to the point that a simple crucial examination is certainly no test of ability or knowledge. They believe in series of practical tests of knowledge and intelligence more from over a period of two or three years. The results of all these tests, they say, should be noticed carefully and taken into account when judging a student's ability. The argument no doubt is true for sure but on the whole it may be said that good students do not usually produce bad results and that negligent students do not generally pass.

It can't be ignored that examinations do exert pressure on the minds of the students who lose all their enthusiasm for life at the approach of an examination. Tutors are engaged, notes and guess-papers are purchased, special lectures are attended, coaching classes get crowded, in short, and all possible measures are taken to get through the examination. The reason for all this is that throughout the term the students pay little attention to their studies taking it lightly for the time and so when a test is near they have to concentrate all their energies on studies and get panic.

The scheme of internal assessment introduced some years ago by some institutions is seen as a step in the direction to keep a watch on the students' work and regularity in their studies. Parents and teachers are the most important people who play crucial role at the time of examinations. They have to build a serious and but interesting environment around their children so that they can study with full attention and focus and achieve success in the examination. And the students have to develop the habit of learning on daily basis to come out of the examination fever.

97

A FAREWELL!

"Goodbyes are not forever. Goodbyes are not the end. They simply mean I will miss you, till we meet again."

The most memorable period of one's lifetime is the time s/he spends in school. No doubt, it is a period of golden era, which one recalls nostalgically for the rest of his/her life. Counting on all those memories of earlier days which seems as if it was yesterday, this golden period of my life came to its sudden end on the 2nd of February, which was my last day at school with everyone.

Since it was the day of parting from my friends, school mates and teachers, the farewell party was heart-breaking, as my educational career in the school was drawing to a close. It was the time to leave for good, my dear school, where I had spent my past ten years of life.

The farewell had to take place in our school ground, decorated with multi-colored clothes, balloons, decorative items and fancy lights. The seats were arranged on the footsteps of the ground.There were chairs for teachers and other inmates of the school also.

Though the ambience was of joy and excitement, yet it had a feel of melancholy and sadness in the air. All out-going students were dressed their best, boys in dashing suits and girls in eye catching dresses and sarees. Everything was perfect! This was the first time in the span of twelve years that I was not wearing my school uniform. Though it was a little weird, but had a feeling of joy. We were welcomed by our juniors at the gate of the school with a small tilak on our forehead. We all occupied our seats and the function started.

The ceremony started with the speech given by our principal.Then came the students of the 11th class, who were hosting the party in our honour. It included mouthwatering, tasty dishes and drinks. After the party, programs of entertainment were put up for amusement and recreation by the hosting party.

Students of class XIth performed by dancing and singing on various songs. An activity which consisted of four rounds involving ramp walk, talent showcase, question answers etc was organized. And at the end four students were awarded with the titles and gifts. Two of them were Mr and Ms Ramjas.

Finally, we were asked to take over the charge of the stage, and then what? The Dance Party started! Everyone was dancing their hearts out, in the name of years of friendship, memories, to the best days and to the best school. We danced with our friends and teachers, took pictures with and autographs of our favourite teachers. It was so much fun!

Teachers too delivered speeches in English and Hindi, which advised us to keep up the name and prestige of the school. Also, to never forget what we have been taught for years, our morals and values. Finally, they all wished us a brilliant success, not only in the forthcoming examination but in actual life also.

This continued till it was the time for the party to break. And then came a moment when we all have to bid adieu to our friends, our teachers and the school, promising each other to always stay in touch with those hidden tears in the eyes. Ruskin Bond has rightly described the movements of parting with a true friend and well wisher,

"You may break; you may shatter the vase, if you will, The smell of the roses shall linger there still"

No one can take away my identity of being a RAMJA-SIAN from me. I will always remain what my school has made me, a true Ramjasian!

MY FAVORITE BOOK

In modern times books are being published in a large number and in variety of subjects. It is not possible for a man to read all books in the world, so everyone has his own taste. Some people think reading books is waste of time but they are wrong. One needs to pick a book of his/her taste. Reading of an irrelevant book can be wastage of time or ruin of one's career. We need to take advice from experts or from our elders. They can tell us better about the usefulness of reading books.

Many books are to be read once or some can be read several times. One of my favorite books is Secret Seven written by Enid Blyton. I don't only like the the book but Enid Blyton is one of my favorite authors. She was born in London on November 28, in 1897. Her first poem was published in 1917 entitled ''Have You''. Her first book was published in 1922 entitled ''Child Whispers''. It is published in 15 volumes.

The Secret Seven which is the first title of the book was published in 1949. Whenever I'm free or get bore I sit and start reading the book. These are series of a mystery book for children in which there is a group of seven friends who are always looking for some kind of adventure.

The Secret Seven is a fictional group of child detectives. The book consists of Peter (society leader), Janet (Peter's sister), Jack Barbara, George, Pam and Colin and most important member Scamper (Peter's dog). Jack's sister Susie and her best friend Binkie often make appearance. Both Susie and Binkie hate Secret Seven and they play tricks to humiliate others. They hold regular meetings to help the community or solve mystery.

The seven has a secret password, a badge and a secret headquarters in garden shed. I like this book because there is a strange twist that I wouldn't think of, so I am always eager to know what it will lead to. The part of Secret Seven that I like the most is ''Shock for the secret seven'' because in this book dogs are disappearing from the village, but the seven are so busy arguing with each other that they don't even notice. Then the poor scamper becomes the latest victim, and its all system goes for the secret seven!

I really enjoy reading this book that I can read it many times. I was really taken in by the Secret Seven, how they solve the mystery and also how Susie and her friend Binkie play tricks on secret seven. I love the way how the plot was built, the stealing of dogs seems a web to draw detectives.

Books have the ability to take you to another world. They take your imagination to the places you've never been. Books may be exciting, scary and thrilling. Books are one's best friend. In solitary movement books are our true companion which gives us interesting and useful information and knowledge.

99

MY SCHOOL

Eight years back when I walked through the welcoming gates of the school, my heart was filled with pride of being a Ramjasian. I feel proud in saying that I was a student of Ramjas School, Pusa Road and will always be. I have spent six very important and amazing years at Ramjas. It seems only yesterday, when we all stood in the ground and played badminton, having fun eating those aloo kachori or manchurian rice in the school canteen, roaming around in free periods, or practicing for the annual function.

Ramjas Institutions were found by Sri Rai Kedar Nath. Ramjas, Pusa Road is running from 6th standard to 12th standard under the guidance and supervision of our lovely principal Mrs. Mohini Bindra. It provides every little thing which a child requires for his growth, physically or mentally. Whether it's about school playground or sports or a library where you can sit and pen down your thoughts and read as much as you want too. A school with best teachers or I should say guides or friends who lead you towards the path of success. Fun activities, annual plays, various competitions like debates, singing, dancing etc. are all a part of Ramjas's education. Camps, treks, trips are organized to maintain that joyful ambience and to make students learn something out of it.

Talking about the education system or say studies, Ramjas students have always performed their 100%. The School results have always been at the top. It has given our country bright and hardworking students who will definitely are making their country as well as their school proud. Ramjas has added many feathers to its cap of glory and one of them is " International School Award" given by the British Council in recognition of its work to bring the wider world into the classrooms.

In the fields of Ramjas, I have honed my talents and realized my potential. Being a part of so many competitions, anchoring inter school debate competition, writing for newspaper and lot more there are a lot of things to do. These activities teach you to value the opinion of others, to balance responsibility, to gain knowledge about different fields, to think, to pour out your words, your thoughts, to dream and to pursue your dreams.

I have always thought of my school as my second home. The last two years, class 11th and 12th have heightened my sense of belongingness and I have made so many beautiful memories and friends who will be there for life time in these two years. My journey through the realms of the school is unforgettable.

What could be more wonderful than the school like Ramjas. School is an inseparable and important part of our lives. It is the place where we learn our first lessons. It teaches us the way to live a life. The time I have spent in Ramjas and the experiences I have gained are very precious and no doubt these experiences will remain with me forever. Ramjas is a doorway to knowledge and a passport to success.

100 RECESS IN THE SCHOOL

"Ten minutes is short if it is a recess and long if it is a punishment"
– Cynthia Lewis

Recess means a time when the students can relax after three or four periods of continuous study. Therefore, every student waits for this period eagerly. The recess period comes in the middle of the school hours and its motive is to allow some free time to the students and as well as the teachers to refresh themselves mentally and physically both.

It is usually seen that the students start to feel bore till the arrival of fourth period. They become inattentive to the lessons and no longer follow the teachers. They start to feel restless as they feel hungry. Therefore, they look forward to the recess period. And as the hunger increases, some of the naughty boys approach the school peon and ask him to ring the bell or while the teacher is teaching they eat their tiffins hiding from the teacher. All this shows that change is badly needed.

As soon as the recess bell rings, all the students close their books and put them in their bags and run out of the class whether the teacher has completed the topic or not or he is still in the class or not. This comes natural as they want to be free for some time, away from the dull atmosphere of the class.

When the students come out in the recess period, they find different ways of relaxation. Some eat their food while others sit on the footsteps of the ground and eat their lunches. Some students don't bring their food with them.

So they eat in the school canteen. While a few students sit in the class and enjoy their food the others enjoy gossiping. Some studious students, who love to study every moment, eat their lunch while studying or revising what the teacher has taught in the last four periods. Some sit in the school lawn enjoying the nature while eating food.

Having satisfied their hunger, students especially girls sit in groups and talk about many things for entertainment. The subject of discussion varies. For girls it can be gossips about new fashion trends, female teachers with attitude, studies etc. For boys it can be about sports, how to complete projects, deciding for plans after school hours etc. Small children play in the playground enjoying their childhood to the fullest. While some students complete their homework sitting in the class.

As soon as the recess period is over, all the joy goes away. Again they have to go their respective classes and study. And the most difficult thing is students are in no mood to study after the entertainment made in the recess.

Recess period has become a regular feature in everyday life which is no doubt important for every student to relax so that they can start fresh. These days there is an interval of half an hour in almost all offices, shops, schools, people are provided half an hour break so that they can relax and enjoy their lunch.

101

SUPERSTITIONS

Your birthday wish will not be fulfilled unless you blow all the candles together. "Don't go out after dark", someone advises an expectant mother. Don't go out the moment after you sneeze, it's unlucky. But touchwood! I am not superstitious.

A famous saying goes – "one man's belief is another man's superstition."

Belief which has no basis in reason is superstition. The word 'superstition' literally means "standing over" something in awe. In religion, superstition means irrational fear of mysterious, and admiration for objects which are not proper objects of worship. In old times, people sacrificed to pacify imaginary gods. Such things can be seen till date in rural areas where people believe in *gurujis, babas* and their magic tricks which are just a way to fool people and earn money.

In my opinion, educated people are also becoming a victim of this. People have developed beliefs in such kind of people and perform their every important task as per what *babas* say and this becomes a medium of earning for such people. This has become a business in India. You will find these babas at every corner asking for money and people give them money because they are scared.

In the Middle Ages in Europe, the belief in witchcraft led to the persecution of poor old women, who were suspected of having sold their souls to the devils. The Spanish Inquisition tortured and burnt thousands of good people, at the bidding of superstition. Though such horrors are not practiced in today's developed and civilized world, but superstitions still exists and produces narrow mindedness, bigotry and needless mental suffering.

Hard to believe and hard to ignore but superstitions are something humans haven't done away with. In this age of scientific wizardry and technological radiance in every possible field, there still exist people with such pessimistic minds who give way to these superstitions. If a black cat crosses your path, you will have an accident or if you break a piece of glass, something unfortunate will happen. If a fakir or baba tells you how bad your Mars and "Shani" are, you will do everything which takes off to set the good period in your life but no one thinks if same amount of hard work and diligence is applied in different aspects of lives, we all would do much better.

However, interesting these things may sound, but there is no proof and evidence to support the occurrence of such unbelievable happenings. It can be called just a coincidence and not good luck or bad luck. Researches have stated that radiations that come from the North Pole can affect the human brain in a negative way specially when a person is off to sleep and all his physical defense is at the lowest, that's why one should not sleep with his head facing the north. There are many more examples which also have some logical reasons behind them and are not superstitions.

Superstition is a thing of darkness: it cannot face the light. It is something imaginary. Therefore, one must have knowledge about the positive and negative aspects and ups and downs in life. As knowledge increases, superstition decreases. The beliefs in superstitions will break the movement you start believe in yourself. And the lock of superstition can only be opened with a key of literacy or power of knowledge.

102

WAITING FOR A BUS

In every big city, bus services are available for the local people to travel from one place to another. It is a cheap transport and saves a lot of money. The city of Delhi is expanding rapidly. People travel from far places to attend offices. Sometimes they have to change two buses to reach their office. People don't feel tired of working for long hours but waiting for a bus is really a hectic.

Last Monday I was waiting for a bus at the bus stand of Vivek Vihar at 8 a.m., waiting for my friends so that we can go to college together. When the bus arrived, gate of the bus opened automatically and the crowd walked down from the bus in which there were factory workers, teachers, students of different schools and colleges, tourists and families going to their respective destinations.

But unfortunately this was not my bus. After a while finally the bus came but what I saw was an old lady trying to enter in the bus. There were so many people trying to enter in the bus, pushing each other. No one noticed that there was an old lady among them and no one had courtesy of letting her go first.

As a responsible man, I raised my voice and everybody looked at me. I asked them if it was their mother or father would they have been doing the same. Everybody kept quiet and I holding her hand helped her walk inside the bus and made her sit on a seat. Till then my friends also came and the bus moved from the stop.

There were many kinds of people in the bus, students, office going people, vendors etc. After another fifteen minutes, some more people entered the bus and it became crowded. When the door closed, I was jammed against the door of the bus. The bus was filled to the brim and there was not even much breathing space. I felt stifled and thought I would suffocate. At the next stop, some people got off and I was able to move. But this made my position even more worse as two huge men got in and I found myself sandwiched between the two of them.

As the bus stopped at traffic lights and then move suddenly, I found myself helpless in the situation. I could not even see where the bus was heading as my view was blocked by the passengers. But I did not get panicked as I had to change the bus. A few stops before the changing point, people of the bus started getting off from the bus and there were no passengers getting in. Soon, there were only about twelve passengers left and I luckily got a seat for the rest of the journey till the changing point. When the bus reached the stop where I had to change, I got down with my friends slowly as the other passengers were also getting down and then again waited for the bus to my college.

103

MY AMBITION IN LIFE

People have their own dreams in life. It is always a good thing to have an ambition in one's life. A person without an aim or ambition in life is an unfortunate person. Without a set aim, a person can achieve nothing in his life. An ambition is an incentive to a person to work hard and to achieve success in life.

Different people have different ambitions. Some persons dream of becoming leaders, politicians and social reformers. Some want to amass wealth, others want to achieve fame and some others want to serve the mankind. There are some people who want to become poets and writers whereas most of the people generally have a desire of becoming doctors, engineers or scientists. Many young boys and girls aspire to become actors and actresses. Thus, ambitions differ from person to person.

My ambition in life is to become a teacher. The idea of simple living and high thinking inspires me to take up this profession. The sole object of my life is to lead a life of simplicity and goodness devoted to the service of others. The good examples set by the great teachers of the past are before me. Their life and works inspire me very much to devote myself to this noble profession.

As a teacher, I want to serve my country in my own humble way. There are a lot of illiterate people in India. Removal of illiteracy is the most urgent need today. The role of a teacher is supreme here. I wish to do what I can to educate my countrymen. I am fully aware of the fact that the teachers in our country are ill-paid. A good teacher is a real friend, philosopher and guide of the students. The teacher removes the darkness of ignorance from the minds of students and fills them with knowledge and noble ideals. I want to fulfil their dream as a teacher. A teacher should be free from corruption. I want to be honest and hard-working in my profession. A teacher should be a model to the students and to the society.

India can develop into a great nation if the problems of illiteracy, corruption, superstition and ignorance are removed. I think that I can do my best to remove these problems in my own little way. The students of today are the citizens of tomorrow. So, I will lay great stress on the character formation of my students. A good teacher is the architect of destiny of the students.

Thus as a teacher I will play my role efficiently in the building of my nation. I have nurtured a love for young children from my childhood. As a teacher I want to help them to widen their outlook by inculcating good values and right knowledge. The company of young children will help me to refresh my thoughts and outlook. I will try to instill noble qualities of service, sacrifice, patriotism and nationalism in my students. I shall also try to inculcate in them a desire to learn the truth and lead a noble and virtuous life.

104

IF I WERE THE PRIME MINISTER OF INDIA

If I were the Prime Minister of India, I would tap all the sources and see that how the money is being utilised in the hands of a few people of the nation at large. Once this huge amount is under the control of the government, the disparity which exists between the rich and the poor, between the haves and the have-nots would disappear. This money can then be used to better the lot of poorer classes. I would give top priority to education, agriculture and setting up of new industries. These schemes would provide food for all, protection against disease and old age and better housing facilities. There would be work for all. Production would increase. Unemployment would disappear. There would be no discontentment. The country would move on the path of progress.

My next step as Prime Minister would be to strengthen the defence of the country. I would see that enough funds are set apart for defence production and maintenance. Ordnance factories would be set up. Aeroplanes, bombers and modern weapons of warfare would be manufactured in India. The armed forces would be equipped with the most sophisticated weapons. The country would be a match for any enemy that dares attack her.

Next I would turn my attention to wipe out corruption, nepotism and favouritism in government offices. I would see that all corrupt officials are punished. I know that this is a difficult work. Some of the party men are likely to be found guilty. I would, however, be very hard on those who are found guilty. I would, surely invite much criticism for this but I would not mind it. I know that the country is with me in my noble work. The office of the Prime Minister is not a bed of roses. The Prime Minister has to tackle many problems. I am sure I would solve these problems one by one.

I shall try to establish a truly socialistic pattern of society. The gap between the rich and the poor will be narrowed down. Nobody will be allowed to hold more than one house. The Right to Property will be taken away. The rich will not be allowed to become richer beyond a certain limit and the poor will be taken away. The rich will not be allowed to become richer beyond a certain limit and the poor will not be allowed to become poorer. Medical treatment will be free for the needy. There will be no unemployment. Agriculture will be given the highest priority. Family planning will be strictly enforced to achieve a target of zero growth. Cottage and small scale industry will grow simultaneously with heavy industries. More and more hydel power projects and solar power sets will be installed so that there is no shortage of power in the country.

Character building has an important role in career development.   Textbooks will be re-written to build up character, a sense of nationalism and patriotism. Every student will be made to feel that he/she is an Indian first and an Indian last. They will be made to participate in constructive activities and will be called upon to build a new India free from poverty, dirt and lethargy. Sports and cultural activities will be encouraged on a big scale. Sportsmen would be caught young and given an intensive training so that they bring a name and fame to the country in various international sports.

Under my able stewardship, the country will march on the greater and greater prosperity. Evils like corruption, smuggling and hoarding will become things of the past. Our country will be a heaven of peace and prosperity. In the international field, India will occupy a place of honour. All this is no bragging or self-praise. Nothing is impossible. I shall do my best to fulfil the dreams of Mahatma Gandhi the Father of the Nation. In a very short time, my country will become a land of peace and prosperity where every head is high, where every hand is busy, and where every heart is happy.

105

MY HOBBY

Hobby is a good thing a person gets from childhood. It can be developed at any age though the best timing is to get from childhood. We all do some kind of work according to our interest which gives us happiness and joy that is called hobby. Some people get different hobbies according to their interest, likes and dislikes. There are many types of hobbies such as dancing, singing, drawing, playing indoor or outdoor game, bird watching, collecting antiques, photography, writing, eating, reading, sports, playing, gardening, music, watching TV, cooking, talking, and so many. Our hobbies help us in earning livelihood and make a successful career. Hobby is something we can fully enjoy in our leisure or free time.

My favourite hobbies are cooking, listening music and gardening however I always prefer gardening. Gardening is like meditation to me, which improves my work efficiency, interest and ability. It gives me high level of peace and makes my whole day useful. Every early morning I enjoy my blooming garden, growing plants slowly on daily basis. I also enjoy sunrise and sunset daily in my garden. I generally like to do my school home work in my evergreen garden. I play badminton with my father daily in the evening in my garden and enjoy evening walk with my mom. I daily watch new developments in plants and do watering. I also try planting new and decorative plants to my garden in order to enhance its look and beauty.

I am 14 years old and want to continue my favourite hobbies till the end of my life. These activities would keep me busy, happy and away from all tensions of daily life. My parents always promote me to continue my hobbies. They become so happy when I take my problems in easy way and try to solve them without getting anger and tension. My mom says that gardening is a good hobby than other ones; it blesses us because we give life to someone through watering and planting new plants. From my childhood I work daily in my garden for one hour to keep it well maintained. I have made there a nice and attractive green carpet using velvet grass. I have prepared beautiful flowerbeds in every corner of the garden and planted colourful roses, lilies, mogra, sunflowers, and other seasonal flowers. At Christmas, I decorate a big Christmas tree in the mid of my garden and enjoy Christmas celebration with my parents and friends.

106

THE PERSON I ADMIRE MOST

I admire a lot of people but the person I admire the most is my mother. She is the most important person in my life. There is no reason for me to live without her by my side. My mom is a church leader. She is a very good leader because she works hard and gives a very good advice. She likes to learn something new. She loves to go to Church at the provinces and teach Bible to the women. She mostly cares all other than herself.

I admire her because she is a very intelligent, good, ambitious and she has many goals in her life. She takes good care of everybody and is also a very helpful leader. She is humble and tries to fit into every class. She is a wonderful mother, very patient, sensitive and open hearted. Whenever people have trouble they come to her for help. She is a great and fun-loving person to hang around because she has a great sense of humour to everybody.

My mother has many talents such as teaching and loving the kids. She is a very good adviser, a good model mother. Generally, my mom is friendly. She is very patient and careful in everything. She always opens her heart to listen to everyone and helps them in need. She always encourages me and makes me happy. She says my dad and me is the most important person in her life that she has to care.

She is very important to me because she has many good things that I have to learn from her. I admire my mom so much and I love her. She always advises me and teach me to walk in the right path. She even teaches me to live life with no regrets every day as to what should I do and how I have to respect to other people.

She is the best gift that god has given to me. I love my mother.

107

IMPORTANCE OF EDUCATION

"The only person who is educated is the one who has learnt how to learn and change" *Oscar Wilde*

Education is the lamp that dispels darkness. "Education is the agent of change. In the contemporary world, it has become a principle aspect of everyone's upbringing. In this millenium, rather than being a luxury, education has become a necessity. Moreover, it does not only equip us with reading, writing and learning skills but also makes us judicious, improves our thinking skills and how to respond in a situation and takes us towards holistic development.

The educational sector is a very large sector in India. It includes primary and high schools, under-graduate and post-graduate colleges, B-schools etc. Though a large part of India still falls under rural sector, the educational institutions at that level include small government and private schools and vocational colleges.

What I believe is that education has made the world a better place to live in as it has civilized the people to be a social being. The people who have chosen the path of education are leading a great successful life and are above the poverty line. Today, education has become the need of everybody's life not only because it boosts up your self confidence but also results in high intellectual level and raises your general awareness. It is also seen that education has helped in solving many problems like child labour, domestic violence, human trafficking etc.

which are posed as grave problems in the society.

Even after eradicating so many evils and problems from the country and serving its people with knowledge so that they can stand on their own feet, it is still believed by some orthodox people that education is nothing but money gone in vain. Education has multifaceted effects on humanity. A child when sent to school for the first time is hesitant but as the time passes by he learns the facts as education infuses in him the spirit to live a successful and respectful life. Education adds to morals and values to the lives of people. Also, it teaches manners and etiquettes which is very important in a person's life to live a disciplined life. Moreover, it makes the democratic system more democratic for educated people are aware about their fundamental rights, policies and schemes. Now they can't be deceived by anyone. More and more people are becoming educated; hence getting the power of self controlling their lives for their own good.

There are many children who want to learn so much through education but their circumstances restrict them from doing so. To overcome this problem, our government has introduced many bills and has made amendments like Right to Education. As per RTE 25% of the students should be from Economically Weaker Section(EWS). Another example is of ''Each one, Teach one'' campaign which was introduced successfully.

Education helps us to understand our past, mistakes we have made and all the things that need to be done to improve our present by working hard, gaining as much knowledge as one can so that one has a bright and successful future ahead. Education works like a tool to unite people living on the mother earth for a better and beautiful world.

Hence, one who hasn't been educated hasn't been refined. I strongly believe that India has a great future ahead as long as people and the government remains united to fight against illiteracy and spread education.

"Education is the most powerful weapon which you can use to change the world" — Nelson Mandela

108

TSUNAMI

Tsunami (seismic sea waves or seismic waves) is one of the most perilous natural calamities. It is a series of waves in a water body that occurs due to the displacement of a huge volume of water in oceans and other water bodies like rivers, lakes, etc. It happens due to earthquakes, volcanic eruptions, landslides and other underwater explosions that cause the seabed to make sudden movements and shift a huge amount of water to the surface. Tsunami Intensity scale, seismometer and Richter scale are some of the devices used to measure the magnitude of seismic or tsunami waves. These waves don't resemble normal sea waves; they have longer wavelengths and stretch over long distances. One of the researches says that about 80 percent of the tsunamis occur in the Pacific Ocean.

The 1896 Japan tsunami and the 2004 Indian Ocean tsunami are amongst the most hazardous natural disasters of all time. The death toll reached to millions. The Indian Tsunami not only affected Indian states like Tamil Nadu and Andhra Pradesh but also neighbouring countries like Indonesia, Thailand, Nepal, Bhutan, etc. As a result of the Japan disaster, the country built numerous tsunami walls and flood gates of height up to or more than 12 metres to protect the densely populated coastal areas and as a precautionary measure, tsunami warning system is also being installed in the Indian Ocean.

Tsunamis can reach up to the heights of 100 feet or more and chase across water bodies at the speed 500 miles an hour. It cannot be prevented but surely be predicted. Many Geologists, oceanographers and seismologists have been successful in predicting tsunami by observing factors like the movement of sea waves and occurrence of earthquakes. Also, tsunami warning systems are used to caution the people living in the nearby areas before the waves hit the ground and earthquake engineering measures are adopted to reduce the destruction caused onshore.

The Indian governments and other regulatory bodies like the NGOs play a significant role in the evacuation process during such natural calamities and have also devised committees like The United Nations Disaster Mitigation Committee that help protect people and give early warning signals to the people. People are advised to stay on higher grounds or floors during a tsunami and return to the shore only when directed by the experts as per the current situations.

Tsunami is a deadly wave that not only annihilates mankind and flora and fauna but also has other consequences such as destruction of property and changes in landscape. Once, it knocks down, it demolishes everything that comes its way starting from the infrastructure to buildings to sweeping away trees, ships, boats, vehicles, etc. and incur massive costs. People living in coastal areas have actually no time to escape and hence, they are worst affected by it. The neighbouring areas too are not able to flee from the brunt of it; floods arise out as an after-effects creating sewage and fresh water problems. Therefore, one must be cautious during the occurrence of such disasters and take precautionary measures to minimise the loss of lives and goods.

SECTION – B
LETTERS

LETTER TO RELATIVES

1. Write a letter to your younger brother advising him to develop reading habits and its importance in the learning process. You are Sara Khan.

Plot No. 245
Rajendra Place
New Delhi
6th October, 2016

Dear Ishita,

Reading books enhances our knowledge on different subject matters. Also, the ability to read has long been recognized as essential to personal fulfilment by UNESCO. Nowadays students just have interest in watching TV, playing games on computer and chatting with the friends. They don't realise the importance of reading. Teachers and parents always try to inculcate good reading habits in us but, we never listen to them and face the consequences later. Even I did when I was in my school and realised it later when it was the time to give entrance tests for getting admissions in good a college.

Wasting the precious time on chatting and playing games won't pay you anything in return. The knowledge we gain from books will surely pay us a bright future in the years to come.

I realise that all work and no play makes jack a dull boy. But, even all play and no work does harm. So, we must always keep a balance between things and have a clear vision about our goals and desires.

I hope, you will understand and take my suggestions and inculcate good reading habits.

Yours lovingly,
Sara Khan

2. Write a letter to your cousin advising her to cope up with examination stress.

Plot No. 87
Vasant Kunj
New Delhi
7th October, 2016
Dear Rahul,

I heard from your mother that your final examinations are approaching soon and you are feeling stressed at this crucial time. Even I used to experience the same when I was in my school. Actually, stress is a common form of anxiety and depression in our day to day life and activities. But, we should always keep in mind that the feeling of stress should never overpower our minds and hearts.

No expression or emotion is greater than the power of our minds, so we must focus on the ability to achieve what we desire in our lives and work hard for it. We all experience stress during exams, during competitions, while meeting deadlines, etc. But, it is nothing to worry about as it happens with everybody and what makes us different from others is our ability to cope up with it.

So, study well for your examinations, not just to come first in the class or meet your parents' expectations but for yourself, your better future.

Yours Lovingly,
Soniya

3. Write a letter to your mother complaining about the poor quality of food served in your hostel.

Student's Hostel No.1
Modern School
Barakhamba Road
New Delhi
May 1st, 20xx

Dear Mother

I hope that you are well and this letter brings a big smile on your face. I know that you will be very angry on me as I could not write a single letter to you or call you for more than a month. But the thing is that I am not keeping well because I have suffered from a very bad stomach infection which has affected my health a lot.

And the cause of my illness is the dirty and stale food which is being served in our hostel. The contractor of our mess is very careless. The food is uncooked most of the times. The curry or rice contains stones etc.

In spite of my friends requests made to the contractor for supplying healthy food, he is supplying the same quality. But now we have brought this matter to the notice of our principal. He has assured us to look into our problems and find solutions for the same as soon as possible.

I shall inform you about the further updates in my next letter. Take care of yours and everyone's health. Lots of love Miss you.

Your loving daughter
Diksha Lodha

4. **Write a letter to your father asking for money**

12/A Janakpuri
New Delhi
May 1st, 20xx

Dear Father

I hope this letter finds you in the best of health.

First of all you do not need to worry about my studies. I am studying well and scoring good marks in every semester. All the teachers are very helpful and give us lots of tasks.

They have given a project which will be executed in the form of an exhibition. And for which we have to make lots of arrangements. In addition I've some money for my best friend's birthday too.

Kindly sent me Rs 3000/- for the same by money order within a week. Convey my respect to mom and to dear Aman.

Your loving daughter
Disha

5. **Write a letter to your father who is away from home telling him how the family has been doing.**

11/A Vasant Kunj
New Delhi
February 6th, 20xx

Dear Father

I am really happy that you are coming in next two days. I hope to see you in good health. Everyone in the family is doing well.

Mother is busy all the time taking care of house and her boutique. Ram is making good progress in his studies. Natasha is going on a trip to Rajasthan organized by her school. It's a three day trip. And I am also busy with my studies.

Hope to see you soon. Lots of love

Your loving son
Sidhartha

6. **Write a letter to your younger brother who has asked for your advice on the choice of profession.**

8/13 Shastri Nagar
New Delhi
June 4th, 20xx

Dear Keshav,

Hello! How are you doing? I hope everyone is doing well. I have just heard from my parents that exams are over and you scored really good percentage. I am really happy and congratulate you on your success.

I got to know that you need my advice regarding the choice of your profession. I don't know about your interests but I know you are a hard-working and passionate person. I suggest you to choose a profession which makes you happy and interests you.

You shouldn't feel that you are doing something which doesn't interest you. For example, I love to cook but my parents wanted me to do engineering. I chose Hotel Management as my career as it interests me and I love doing it.

At last I can just say and advise you to make your career in a field which you think is suitable for you and brings success to you.

Hope to see you soon. All the best for your future.

Your loving brother
Sharad

7. Reply accepting the invitation

Mr. Mani Tandon thanks Ms. Gayatri Chetal for inviting him to a tea party on Wednesday, 5th September, 2016 at 5 p.m. at Clay Oven in Patel Nagar. He takes pleasure in accepting the invitation.

Reply declining the invitation

Mr. Mani Tandon thanks Ms. Gayatri Chetal for inviting him to a tea party on Wednesday, 5th September, 2016 at 5 p.m. at Clay Oven in Patel Nagar.

He will/shall not be able to attend the tea party because of prior unavoidable engagements. He is sorry for not attending the party.

LETTER TO FRIENDS

1. **Write a letter to your friend sharing your experience of the fair.**

89/F, Vasant Vihar
New Delhi
11th September, 20xx

Dear Sapna,

Hi, hope you are doing good and keeping up in good spirits. I recently visited the International Book Fair held at Pragati Maidan and it was an amazing experience. Books of all languages and genres catering to different age groups and tastes were available at the fair. Reading enthusiasts had stuck to the stalls as bees to honey. Not only this, the theatres at Pragati Maidan offered live dance performances and plays based on famous novels and dramas.

Famous authors and poets had also come to the fair. They talked about the salient features of their publications and writings to the interested parties. I brought three books authoring Sydney Sheldon and one for you written by Chetan Bhagat named, Three Mistakes of my life. I really hope you like it.

Hope to see you soon!

Yours lovingly,
Naina

2. **Your friend Nikita, who lives in Agra has got admission in a prestigious college of South Delhi. She wrote to you making enquiries about the hostel accommodation in Delhi.**

    Write a letter to your friend in response to her enquiries.

455/A, Laxmi Nagar
New Delhi
11th September, 20xx

Dear Nikita,

This is in response to the letter you wrote to me about the hostel accommodation in Delhi. I asked a lot of my friends and other acquaintances about the hostel facility in South Delhi and they told me that minimum rent for any hostel is expected to be Rs. 10,000 including three meals per day. The rooms are fully air conditioned and each room has a capacity of two beds. Facilities like refrigerator and washing machine are also provided in the said cost. However, you will be required to give advance rent prior to shifting.

The landlord stays on the same floor and keeps a regular check on the tenants. Boys are not allowed inside the hostel and also girls are required to be back till 10:00 pm. You won't have the freedom to stay out late night for parties and hard drinks are strictly not allowed inside the hostel.

Meanwhile, I will keep on searching for more options, do share your concerns if any.

Yours affectionately,
Nidhi

3. **You are Vikrant/Sakshi. Your friend Rakesh scored poorly in the half yearly examination. Write a letter to him advising him to work hard and motivate him for a better performance.**

Plot No. 9
Vaishali, Ghaziabad
U.P.
7th October, 2016

Dear Rakesh,

Hope you are keeping up in good spirits and health. I heard that you didn't score well in the half yearly examinations. But, we all know that you are a brilliant and hard-working student. Therefore, the news I got is unbelievable and shocking.

One failure is not the end of life. Life goes on and so do the problems, happiness and grief. Everything is a part and parcel of life. There is no need to lose heart as failures are the pillars to success. So, I would like you to concentrate on the final examinations and study harder for it.

The examinations test our knowledge about the subjects taught in school but, remember no test is greater than life. We must never lose hope and always work hard to achieve what we want.

Yours lovingly,
Sakshi

4. You are Vrinda. Write a letter to your friend Abhiratha, telling him the dangers of drug addiction. Give him some catchy warnings too.

Plot No.67, Vaishali
Ghaziabad
U.P.
20th September, 20xx

Dear Abhiratha,

I recently heard from one of our mutual friends that you had a break up and soon after you started consuming drugs and alcohol. This is totally insane. You should not consume these substances or one day they will lead you straight to the door of the hospital. Now-a-days, drug addiction is the major cause of deaths and it majorly happens amongst the younger generations which start consuming alcoholic substances due to peer pressure or study pressure. But, one should understand that this is not the ideal solution to it.

Drug addiction is a brain disease because the abuse of drugs leads to changes in the structure and function of the brain. I realise that the habit cannot be left immediately but I would want you to understand that it is high time that you should at least start minimising its consumption.

Many people mistakenly see drug abuse and addiction as social problem and may characterize the addicted as morally weak. Drugs are a curse to the society so I hope to see positive changes in you in the near future.

Yours affectionately,
Vrinda

5. **Write an informal invitation to a friend for a cinema show.**

D 6 Narmada Apartments
Vasant Kunj
New Delhi
August 1st, 20xx

Dear Diksha,

I hope you are well and happy there. I am good too. As our end term exams are over, we have some free time to enjoy these days. I was also making a list of the activities that we can do as it's a time for relief, rest and recreation.

So, I was thinking how about going for a movie? I guess it will be a fun. We can go to watch Rustomon August 31st, 20xx at any theatre of your or my choice. I have heard about a movie. It's a romantic murder mystery and I guess it will be perfect to start our holidays together. We can meet at Rajeev Chowk Metro Station at 12 p.m. Hope to hear a positive reply soon.

Your loving friend
Gayatri

6. **Write a letter to your friend inviting him to your sister's wedding.**

16/8 Patel Nagar
New Delhi-05
October 30th 20xx

Dear Manish

I hope you are healthy and happy there. I am good too. I am writing this letter to inform you that my sister Ria is getting married and the wedding is being solemnised on 30th October 20xx

The marriage will be held at G.K garden Vasant Kunj. I would love if you will come to attend this wedding at least four days earlier so that you can enjoy every little thing and help us in arrangements.

I will be very happy if you come. Please do message the date and time you will be coming on so that I can come and pick you from airport.

Many functions will take place and it will be a super fun and you have to stay for at least a week or more. Once again I invite you and your family on this special occasion. I hope you will come

Give my regards to your parents.

Your sincerely
Naman

7. **Write a letter to your friend showing sympathy on his failure in the examination.**

19/An Old Street
Indore
October 2nd , 20xx

Dear Diksha

I was shocked to know about your failure in second end term examination. My eyes could not believe when I saw your result on internet.

I know that you have worked very hard for the examination and no doubt you are an intelligent girl. Your practical attitude, your knowledge speaks about you.You were the top ranker in entrance examination. All along, you have been a diligent student.

But this result has made you unhappy. I know you were disturbed because of few reasons and your bad health but you have to forget everything and stand again and work hard to secure good results next time and make your parents feel proud.

Do not take this failure to heart. Take it as a lesson and I am sure you would surely perform better in the coming examinations.

Please convey my warm regards to your parents and love to younger brother.

Yours sincerely
Gayatri

8. Write a letter to your friend to convey your condolence on the death of his mother.

2A/16 Chawari Bazar
Old Delhi
September 5th, 20xx

Dear Tarak,

I recently heard the news of sudden demise of your mother. I am still not able to believe that she is no more. A month back we enjoyed your birthday party at your house and enjoyed the delicious food made by aunty and now this news has left me in total shock.

This is no doubt an inseparable loss. Mothers are angels sent by God to take care of us life-long. And she was a very fine lady who treated me not less than his son. I enjoyed her company, food made by her a lot.

I know this moment is unbearable for you. You and your family have lost its most precious jewels. But I request you to be strong and become a support of your family because they need you the most this time.

I send my heartfelt condolence to the entire family in this situation of sorrow.

With deep sympathies

Yours sincerely
Kunal

LETTER TO PRINCIPAL

1. Write a letter to the Principal of your school requesting him to bring about some improvements in the school library.

560, Mayur Vihar
New Delhi
12th September, 20xx

The Editor
St. Xavier's School
New Delhi

Subject: Improvement in School Library

Respected Sir/Madam,

I am the Head girl of the school and I want to bring to your kind notice that the condition of the school library is very unsatisfactory. It is a matter of great concern that the library, storehouse of knowledge doesn't equip the latest version of books and other reading materials.

The shelves are covered with dust and most of the pages of the books are torn. The books are in a very bad condition. Also, the students are not provided with proper seating arrangements.

The students with depressing financial backgrounds, who rely on the library as the only source of additional knowledge, are the worst affected. Ma'am, I request you to look into the matter and take necessary steps as soon as possible.

Yours Obediently,
Nikita Sharma
(Head Girl)

2. Write an application to your school Principal, requesting him/her to include ECA period in the time-table for one hour daily.

560, Nirman Vihar
New Delhi
18th September, 20xx

The Editor
St. Thomas School
New Delhi

Subject: Inclusion of ECA (Extra Curricular Activities) period in the time-table

Sir/Madam,

I am the Sports Captain of the school and this is to bring to your kind notice that the students don't even get one hour a day for physical exercise while their mental exercise continues for the whole day. One hour ECA (Extra Curricular Activities) period must be added to their time-table in order to make no jack a dull boy.

It will not only boost the talent of the students but also will rejuvenate and re-energise them for their daily schedules. ECA plays a very vital role in the students' life. It not only motivates them to study more but also helps them explore their area of interests and realise their passions.

Moreover, nowadays children are only restricted to indoor video games and online surfing, lack of outdoor games make them physically weak. Thus, I would like you to look into the matter and take suitable steps.

Yours obediently,
Nikita Sharma'
(Head Girl)

3. **Write an application to the principal of your school for grant of leave on the occasion of your sister's marriage.**

16/18 W.E.A
Padam Singh Road
Karol Bagh
New Delhi – 110005
26thOctober, 20xx

The Principal
Ramjas School
Pusa Road
New Delhi – 110005

Sub: Application for Marriage Leave

Sir,

I would like to inform you that my sister is getting married on 19th December, 20xx and I have to attend the ceremonies.

Therefore, I request you to grant me leave for one week that is from 14th December to 20th December so that I may be able to attend the ceremonies/functions.

Thanking you
Yours obediently
Gayatri Chetal
Class – XII B – Comm.

4. **Write an application to the principal of your school for the grant of scholarship to continue your studies.**

16/18 W.E.A.
Padam Singh Road
Karol Bagh
New Delhi-110005

4thJanuary, 20...
The Principal
St. Thomas School
New Delhi

Sub: Application for Scholarship

Dear Sir

With due respect, I beg to say that I belong to a lower middle class family. My father who used to earn and look after all our needs can no more earn as he is suffering from severe paralysis attack.

This situation has bought financial crisis in our family. My mom can earn an amount which helps in feeding the entire family. As per the situation, it is becoming difficult for me to continue my education.

Besides being a good and intelligent student, I have participated in many competitions and won many prizes.

I would be thankful if you can kindly grant me a merit-cum-means scholarship. I hope you will understand my problem. Your kindness would allow me to continue my studies and fulfil my dream of becoming a great journalist.

Thanking you!

Yours obediently
Yash Raj
Class IXth-B

5. Write a farewell letter to the principal of your school after leaving the school.

Sector-2, Vaishali
Ghaziabad
Uttar Pradesh

Subject: Application for School Leaving Certificate

Respected Ma'am,
I, Kavita Tripathi of the out–going batch would like to express my gratitude to you. With warm wishes I would like to thank you for the kind support provided by you. It was you who gave me encouragement and without the entire teacher's support I wouldn't have chosen the right track.

You were the one who showed the way to my class room on my first day to school and it's all because of you and your staff that I could fare well in my exams and turned out to be one of the well behaved and a good disciplined student. I will be missing all my teachers and the non-teaching staff for my entire life ahead. Our schooling is the first stage to success and I think I have made it. Once again I express my gratitude for all your support.

Thanking you!

Yours respectfully
Kavita Tripathi

BUSINESS LETTER

1. Write an application for the post of Computer Engineer.

16/18 W.E.A
Padam Singh Road
Karol Bagh
New Delhi-110005
11th March, 20xx

The Manager
Shivang Software
Patel Nagar

Subject: Application for the post of computer engineer

Sir,

With reference to your advertisement in the Times of India dated 9/03/16, for the post of Computer Engineer, I would like to apply for the same.

If given an opportunity, I would like to work for your organisation to the best of my abilities. I am sending my bio data with the application.

Thanking You!

Yours sincerely
Gayatri Chetal

LETTER TO EDITOR

1. Write a letter to the Editor of an English newspaper showing your concern on education beyond classroom teaching.

House No. 314/B, Sarita Vihar
New Delhi
4th September, 20xx

The Editor
The Times of India,
New Delhi

Subject: Education beyond classroom teaching

Dear Sir,

The present education system of India, which implies classroom teaching as its one important ingredient, is not enough for students to succeed in their lives. Theoretical exposure of subjects is not sufficient for the students to understand the concepts; schools must engrain practical exposure in the educational system to help students understand practical working of theories taught in the classes.

Education must therefore take place outside the classes. It should include compulsive training sessions, factory visits, etc. The students should not be confined to only books as a source of knowledge.

Many professional fields like journalism, Information Technology and architecture cannot be mastered just by theoretical knowledge, one needs to have the required technical and physical skill which can only be done through practical exposure. e.g., one cannot learn to speak fluently just by learning how to speak.

Therefore, I hope you will look into the matter and help India reform its education system to brighten the future of generations to come.

Yours faithfully,
Pratibha Katariya

2. Write a letter to the Editor of local newspaper expressing your views on more efficient ways of protesting than in a rowdy manner.

House No. 90, Karol Bagh
New Delhi
7th September, 20xx

The Editor
The Times of India,
New Delhi

Subject: Efficient ways of public protests

Sir,

Through the column of your esteemed newspaper, I would like to bring to the kind notice of you and your readers that the banners which impulse mango people to come on the roads and protest in ruthless and illegal ways. These protests might sound seem to be very attractive on screens but are actually examples of irresponsibility of citizens.

Thus, in order to bring crucial matters of concern in notice of higher authorities, the protests should not be the only way, rather press conferences, group discussions, etc. must be held between authorities and the people in order to reach out to an appropriate solution.

Protests not only disrupt the mind-set of civilians but also the working of the economy.

I hope you will help us bring the matter to the concern to the people and authorities.

Yours faithfully,
Surveen

3. Write a letter to the Editor of a local newspaper on the reaction of general public towards the issue of Child Abuse and what needs to be done to wipe out this problem from the world.

Flat No. 90, Laxmi Nagar
New Delhi
11th September, 20xx

The Editor
The Mumbai Times
Mumbai

Subject: Concern over the Child Abuse

Sir,

The instances of child abuse are increasing at an alarming rate. Children are pitilessly beaten, forced to work and do household chores instead of providing them with a life they deserve they can play, study and enjoy.

Children are emotionally, physically, mentally and sexually harassed on daily basis. This not only hampers their physical and mental growth but also forces them to the point of suicides because they are too afraid to speak to their elders about the harassment.

Maltreated children may grow up to be maltreating adults. A 1991 study indicated that 90 percent of maltreating adults were maltreated as children. Almost 7 million American infants receive child care services, such as day care, and much of that care is poor. Also, many NGOs and governmental organisations are working towards the cause.

Hence, I would like you to pay attention to the graveness of the matter and take suitable measures to curtail the problem.

Yours faithfully,
Nalini Pandey

LETTER OF COMPLAINTS

1. **Write a letter to the dealer complaining about the problem and requesting him to get the defect rectified. Also request him to replace it, if needed against the warranty that goes with it.**

72, Calengute

Goa

11th September, 20xx

The Proprietor

Electronics House

Candolim Road, Goa

Subject: Complaint about defective delivery of Samsung LCD television

Sir,

I am a regular customer of your store and it was two months ago that I purchased Samsung LCD television from your 'Electronics House', Candolim Road, with a warranty of two years, worth Rs. 1, 20,000. But, as soon as I started using it, I found out that the picture was blurred and sound was defective also. Within just two months of the purchase, the television got damaged.

And when I tried to adjust the sound and picture options, the scenario worsened. The colours faded and the sound started to blurt. My family is crazy about television, specially my wife and due to this she missed several programmes.

As the television is in warranty, I would like you to replace it if the defects don't get fixed.

Yours sincerely,
Ankit Sharma

2. **Write a letter of complaint to the manager of the shoe house asking for replacement of defective delivery of shoes at their cost.**

Flat No. 90, Shastri Nagar
Meerut
11th September, 20xx

The Manager
Footsteps Shoe House
Meerut

Subject: Complaint about defective delivery of shoes

Sir,

I am a resident of Meerut and purchased a pair of Woodland shoes vide cash memo no. 1414 dated 19th August, 20xx priced at Rs. 12,000. The salesman showed me the pair I wore them and satisfactorily asked him to pack it for me.

But, as soon as I reached home and unpacked the box to wear shoes for an occasion I found out that both the shoes were meant for the left foot. This callous attitude of your employees is inexplicable. It is not expected from a famous brand like yours.

If this continues, all the customers will lose faith in the brand and ultimately the goodwill of the brand will end. Thus, I am returning the shoes for the replacement at your cost.

Yours sincerely,
Gautam Pandey

3. **Write a letter to the Health Officer complaining against the poor sanitary conditions of street you live in.**

13 A Chinna Market
New Delhi
July 17th, 20xx

The Health Officer
Municipal Corporation of Delhi
New Delhi

Dear Sir

I want to draw your attention towards the poor sanitary conditions of the street I live in. The moment one enters the street has to see a big bin area which is not at all clean. Garbage lies here and there in the street and one has to inhale bad odour and due to which mosquitoes breed.

Roads are broken and have not been repaired from long time. At the time of rainfall, water gets collected in pot holes everywhere, which results in diseases like malaria and cholera.

I have already brought this miserable condition of my street to the sanitary inspector of this locality but no action has been taken so far.

I request you to look into the matter as soon as possible as it can result in bad health of the people and make the locality look worst.

Thanking you!

Yours faithfully
Naren

MISCELLANEOUS

1. Write a letter to the superintendent of police reporting a case of theft.

16/ 18 W.E.A.
Padam Singh Marg
Karol Bagh
New Delhi-110005
August 23rd, 20xx

The Superintendent of Police
West Delhi District
New Delhi

Dear Sir

I wish to report a case of theft which took place two days ago. It was Monday and I and my family went to Mama's house to celebrate *Raksha Bandhan*. For the whole day we were there.

At 8 p.m. we came back home. What we saw was all locks of our home had been broken. After we checked the whole house, we found that Rs 20,000 and some of our expensive assets like Television, CD player, and watches were also taken away.

It is very shocking to see that thieves carried out such a big robbery in the broad daylight though there are so many shops around our house.

    My father registered the case at the local police station but no action has been taken yet.

    I hope that you would immediately look into the matter.

Yours faithfully
Manish

SECTION – C
E-MAILS

E-MAIL TO RELATIVES

1. Write an email to your sister who is out of country telling her how you celebrated Diwali.

To: ABC@gmail.com

From: XYZ@gmail.com

CC: BCD@gmail.com

BCC: NML@gmail.com

Subject : How I celebrated Diwali

Hi Mona,

Thought I'd send a picture of my little monsters. They had a great time celebrating Diwali yesterday. They burnt crackers, lit *diyas*, helped me in the decoration and ate like big giants. No doubt they were missing *massi* there.

Hope you are enjoying with your family in Singapore. Do send me pictures in your reply. Waiting for you to come back so that we can hang out.

Give my love to Rahul and Tina and regards to Sanjeev. Hope to see you all soon.

With love

Pooja

E-MAIL TO FRIENDS

1. **Write an e-mail to a friend sharing with her the experiences of enjoyment.**

To: ABC@gmail.com
From: XYZ@gmail.com
CC: BCD@gmail.com
BCC: NML@gmail.com

Subject: Enjoying my summer vacations

Hi Alisha

My summer vacations weren't boring this time! They were quite adventurous...We went to Jammu and I learnt skiing there! u know it has always fascinated me and I was skiing in real... We had lots of fun there in trekking too!

I will tell u more after returning, it was a memorable experience. And now tell me about your visit.

With love
XYZ

BUSINESS E-MAIL

1. Write an E-mail to your boss asking him about the delay in your promotion.

To: AbhishekSharma@gmail.com
From: HimanshuGauri@Yahoo.com

Subject: Queries about delayed promotion

Hello Sir,

I have been a member of the organisation for seven years now and I have put in my 100 percent in order to excel in the professional environment and achieve organisational goals. I had applied for an Internal Job Posting two weeks before but have not received any responses yet. I have qualified all the four rounds and scored well. Also, I have the required skills and educational qualification for the post. I have also worked as a trainer before.

So, I hope you will look into to the delay in decision making and offer the opportunity to me.

Thanks and Regards,
Himanshu Gauri
(Assistant Trainer)

2. **Write an E-mail to the H.R. of XYZ Pvt. Ltd. for the job opportunity that you saw in the advertisement you read in the newspaper for job application.**

To: NikitaSharma@gmail.com
From: JatinKhurana@Yahoo.com

Subject: Application for the post of Assistant Manager

Hello Sir/Ma'am,

I read your advertisement in the Times of India for the post of an Assistant Manager.

Currently, I am working with ABC company as an Assistant manager in the sales department and I have trained several batches and migrated processes as well. I have the required educational qualification and skills. I also have expertise in the field of marketing and have incorporated various successful marketing strategies into the organisation.

My work has been appreciated by my seniors and I am determined to do well in the future.

My resume is attached. Please let me know if I have to provide you with any further information on my background and qualifications.

I look forward to hear from you. Thank you for your favourable consideration.

Thanks and regards,
Jatin Khuaran

3. **You are the sports secretary of your school. Write a letter to a sport's dealer asking for information regarding sports items that your school wishes to purchase.**

To: dhawansports@outllook.com
From: schoolofheritage@info.com

Subject: Enquiry about the purchase of sports items for school

Dear Sir/Madam,

Our school has recently formed a sports club, and we wish to make the following purchases:

1. Thirty hockey sticks and five hockey balls.

2. Ten badminton rackets and two dozen shuttlecocks.

3. Five footballs.

4. Two complete cricket kits: bats, balls, wickets (stumps), etc.

Kindly send us detailed information about the price, discount for schools, time taken for delivery and the mode of payment.

We will appreciate if you could send us your the latest catalogue. We need these items immediately and look forward to a quick revert.

Yours faithfully,
Faheem Khan
Tel: 99043612

E-MAIL OF COMPLAINTS

1. **Write an email to the Superintendent of Police of your district complaining about the misbehaviour of roadways bus conductor.**

To: spghaziabad@gmail.com
From: karanarora@gmail.com

Dear Sir/Ma'am

Subject: Complaining about the Misbehaviour of Roadways Bus Conductor

I am writing to inform you of the misbehaviour of one of bus conductors of Uttar Pradesh State Road Transport Corporation. In the evening on Tuesday, 1st November, I rode on the bus number 8 line near Main market at Vaishali. I ride this bus for home from work every day, so I am well acquainted with bus conductor, Gagan. But, there was a new bus conductor this evening.

My stop is at Main Market, so I asked the conductor for a ticket of Rs. 10 as I always do. At my stop, I was just going to get down from the bus while the checking authority came and asked me for my ticket. Since the conductor gave me the ticket of higher value though I paid him the same amount as usual, I was panicked. The conductor got down and ran away taking all the cash money with him.

I do not know the name of this bus conductor but he had black hair and wore a gold earring. I sincerely hope that you will take appropriate action to reprimand the conductor. I would appreciate if you can call me at 555-555-5555 at your earliest convenience for follow-up information.

Yours Sincerely,
Karan Arora

2. **Write an email to the Chief Medical Officer drawing his attention towards prevention of viral diseases like Chikungunya and Dengue.**

To: cmonewdelhi@gmail.com
From: raadhikaroy@gmail.com

Subject: Prevention of viral diseases like Chikungunya and Dengue

Dear Sir,

Mosquitoes have become a menace in our locality these days. As soon as the night comes, mosquitoes attack us from around.. The viral diseases like Cikunguniya and dengue are spreading rapidly because of mosquito bites. People are trying to protect themselves through mosquito nets and mosquito coils. Yet, they do not get rid of mosquitoes.

It is high time when the government needs to do something to alleviate mosquito menace. Anti-mosquito chemicals should be sprayed. Stagnant pools of water should be cleaned. Also people should come forward to help the government and alleviate the mosquito hazard.

I hope you will look into the matter and make people aware about the fatal risks of mosquito bites and help them to prevent the disease for the safety and sound health of the people.

Yours sincerely,
Raadhika Roy

3. Write an email to the chairman of a Central Board of Film Certification asking him or her not to release the films that show vulgarity in Hindi movies and deform the Indian culture.

To: chairman@CBOFC
From: ABC@gmail.com
CC: BCD@gmail.com
BCC: NML@gmail.com

Subject: Vulgarity in Hindi Movies

Gone were the days when parents and elders could sit together to watch a movie with their children. With the passage of time, Hindi movies contain much western culture and adult contents and it becomes difficult for parents to watch the movie with their children. In addition to the action and drama, the vulgarity shown has no extremes in today's movies.

India has always been known for its culture and secularism. However, there are a few movies based on our culture. The media is trying to reflect on the obscenity shown in films and raising concerns on this issue. The movies that show extreme violence, murder, and sexual assault cause mental harm to children. Teenagers and youths try to apply the same trends in their daily life and get distracted from the path of glory and nobility. Most of the movies show extreme drama which may hurt sentiments of people. The movies which show comedy, most of the times overdo the humour by making a mockery of reality.

Therefore, I request you not to pass the movies that distort the basic theme of our cultural values. The movies that are extremely entertaining, based on culture, religion etc. without hurting the sentiments of any community and that do not show vulgarity in cinema and deform the Indian culture be allowed to do the business.

Yours Truly
ABC

4. Write an email to the editor of a newspaper drawing attention towards crimes against women and children. Also provide some Helpline of NGOs and governmental agencies for emergency situations.

26.11.xxxx

To: editor45@newstimes.com
From: Shekhar Malhotra@gmail.com
CC: BCD@gmail.com
BCC: NML@gmail.com

Sub: Crimes Against Women and Children

Dear Sir,

Through the columns of your esteemed daily, I would like to express my feelings about the safety of women and children. Every day, we come across news headlines about sexual assault, molestation, sexual harassment, rapes, trafficking, ill treatment of women in houses, violence against women in remote areas etc. At many places the children under the age of 14 are employed in risky and hazardous environment in factories and are sexually harassed at work place and in the community. It seems that criminals are no longer afraid of the law.

Therefore, we must apply remedial or curative measures such as fast track courts especially dedicated to deal only with such offences and crimes. The stricter laws should be made so that nobody can imagine of doing such crimes. It is time when the government should undertake drastic measures to put an end to crime against women and children.

So, I appeal people to give equal respect and security to women and request you to provide some helpline of governmental agencies and of NGOs for emergency situations.

Yours Truly,
Shekar Malhothra

5. **Write an email to the editor of a national newspaper drawing attention of the community towards bad condition of roads in their locality.**

To: editor@timesofindia.com
From: Janakakumara@gmail.com

Subject: Drawing Attention of the Community towards Bad Condition of Roads

Dear Sir

I want to draw attention of the community and yours towards bad condition of roads in our locality, Ghaziabad. We have made several complaints to the concerned authority but none paid a little attention. For the last four months the road has been almost impassable and it has been neglected. The surface of the road is broken by heavy rains. There are heaps of rubbishes on both sides of the road. They leave only little space in the middle. During the rainy season, the road gets flooded even after little showers. There are potholes on the road. The broken culvert is also a danger for vehicles especially at night. This road serves a large number of houses in this area. There is a lot of traffic along the road at any time of the day. So we shall be grateful to you to draw the attention of negligent authority and the community as well.

Yours Truly,
Janaka Kumara